THE WRITERS OF MONTREAL

The Writers of Montreal

ELAINE KALMAN NAVES

Véhicule Press

MONTRÉAL

Published with the assistance of The Canada Council.

Photo and illustration research: Nancy Marrelli
Printing: Imprimerie d'Édition Marquis Ltée
Photo of the author: Allen McInnis, *Montreal Gazette*

CANADIAN CATALOGUING IN PUBLICATION DATA
Naves, Elaine Kalman
The writers of Montreal

Includes bibliographical references.
ISBN 1-55065-045-9

Authors, Canadian--Quebec--Montréal--Biography
I. Title
PS8081.N38 1993   C810.9'971428   C93-090668-3
PR9186.2.N38 1993

Published by Véhicule Press, P.O.B. 125, Place du Parc Station,
Montreal, Quebec, Canada H2W 2M9

Distributed in Canada by General Distribution Services,
30 Lesmill Road, Don Mills, Ontario M3B 2T6.

Printed in Canada on acid-free paper.

For Gary, Jessica and Rebecca

Contents

Epidemic Outbursts of Poetry and Fiction

Preface

WHEN I BEGAN RESEARCHING the first set of Writing Montreal columns for the *Montreal Gazette* in the spring of 1992, a librarian whom I consulted arched a graceful eyebrow.

"Montreal writers? There are none!" Then, under her breath as an afterthought, she added, "Well..., perhaps Hugh MacLennan."

Little did she know. Over the course of two summer seasons, the problem proved to be one of an overabundance, not a shortage, of literary blessings. The only way *Montreal Gazette* Books Editor Bryan Demchinsky and I found to contain the project in its first year was to limit the series (originally intended to run for six weeks) to sixteen articles about dead authors who had written in English and French!

The popularity of the original series led to a sequel featuring living writers the following year.

The essays contained in *The Writers of Montreal* don't aspire to be the last word in either biography or criticism. Inspired originally by Montreal's 350th birthday, they seek to capture the essence of the lives and careers of selected writers. Neither scholarly, nor exhaustive, these profiles really only scratch the surface of the energetic literary life of Montreal.

Plenty of room remains for additional series and columns. In particular, I would have liked to include brilliant Montrealers who wrote/write in languages other than French or English (such as the renowned Yiddish poet Rachel Korn, and the novelist Yehuda Elberg) and regret that many distinguished writers who qualified under all our criteria for inclusion were nevertheless left out. Victor-Lévy Beaulieu, Jacques Ferron, Louis Hémon, Louise Maheux-Forcier, Brian Moore spring immediately to mind. But there are many others, particularly of a younger generation of talented writers.

I would also have preferred if the standards for inclusion had been

100 per cent scientific. Informal criteria for the author roster were headed by excellence in writing, a physical connection to the city, and some links with it in subject matter as well.

In recent years, a gratifying number of writers with international reputations (Marie-Claire Blais, Leonard Cohen, Mavis Gallant, Naïm Kattan, Irving Layton, Mordecai Richler and Michel Tremblay, among others) have done the city proud. Nonetheless, literary history and civic pride make incompatible bedfellows. Though this collection of essays reaches back to the earliest colonial times, it should be made immediately clear that, until the soaring but tragically short career of poet Émile Nelligan at the turn of the twentieth century, none of the city's writers scaled literary heights.

Which is not to say that the emerging strains of writing do not yield plenty to interest and, at times, even to titillate the reader. And so, since the original project began with a view of paying homage to Montreal's literary past, I thought it important to sample these earliest examples of local writing. Thus, in Part One—which I have entitled "From Cartier's Hochelaga to MacLennan's *Two Solitudes*"—cheek by jowl with portraits showcasing the city's former literary greats (obvious choices: Émile Nelligan, A.M. Klein, Stephen Leacock, Gabrielle Roy and Hugh MacLennan), are some lesser, as well as lesser-known, literary lights.

Because there were few professional writers to speak of until the middle of the nineteenth century, I looked for pioneers beyond the field of *belles lettres*: in the Church, and among politicians, orators and journalists. Some of these pioneers wrote with energy and skill. Others were heavy-footed in the extreme.

Perhaps the most rewarding aspect of my research was uncovering some obscured careers. The little-known Rosanna Leprohon, for instance, was immensely popular well beyond her lifetime. (She wrote in English, but her books reached a wide readership in French.) It's likely no coincidence either that another bestselling and overlooked author, Gwethalyn Graham, was also a woman.

I have borrowed the title of Part Two of this book— "Epidemic Outbursts of Poetry and Fiction"—from writer and academic Hugh Hood. The careers of the fifteen authors in this section may be more familiar to readers as, happily, these writers are all alive, kicking and, for the most part, still writing. As with the authors of the past, here too I have tried to find the telling biographical details that shed light on the literary works.

In this regard, I am grateful for in-depth interviews granted me by Yves Beauchemin, Marie-Claire Blais, Nicole Brossard, Roch Carrier, Louis Dudek, Naïm Kattan, Irving Layton, Jovette Marchessault and Michel Tremblay, and for telephone interviews with Gratien Gélinas and Mordecai Richler.

I am indebted to Bryan Demchinsky, the *Montreal Gazette*'s Books Editor, for conceiving the idea of the "Writing Montreal" columns and for assigning the series to me. He both edited and mentored the project from beginning to end, and was unflaggingly generous with his time and patience.

A big thank you to Simon Dardick, publisher of Véhicule Press, for turning the columns into a book and for including *The Writers of Montreal* in his special 20th anniversary list.

Finally, I owe thanks to my husband Gary for his loving support and encouragement in this as in (almost) all of my enthusiasms over the years.

I hope that this book will be viewed as an introduction to, not a summation of, Montreal's literary life. And that it will stimulate further interest in the city's writers and their writings.

Elaine Kalman Naves
Montreal, October 1993

INTRODUCTION

An Abundance of Literary Blessings

There is nothing more magical than admiring the
thinking and emotion of creators."
—NICOLE BROSSARD

"'Do you think you'll ever understand
the soul of this city...?'"
—YESHIM TERNAR, "Indigo"

Lissen, me I'm no tête-carrée
Born in an ice cube tray.
Anglo-a-go-go or no,
Da solitudes will always stay
At two:
Icemakers 'n' icebreakers.
Which one are you?
—RAYMOND FILIP, "Bling"

MONTREAL IS UNIQUE in the world in possessing a rich literary heritage in both English and French. But—for idiosyncratic reasons that cut to the city's very heart—as Hugh Hood has put it so astutely, "Anybody who lives in Montreal, whatever his language, sees himself from time to time as a member of a minority."

The subtext beneath the biographical essays that comprise the bulk of *The Writers of Montreal* is the literary life of this city with a divided soul.

Its pre-eminence as the centre of French-Canadian letters began relatively late. Until the last quarter of the nineteenth century, Quebec City was the literary leader, the shift to Montreal becoming evident in 1877 when Louis Fréchette, the most prominent poet of the day, moved to Montreal from Quebec. By 1895 a group of university students had founded the École littéraire de Montréal, a literary society fitfully active for some four decades, whose glory days in 1898-99 encompassed the enthralling poetry readings of Émile Nelligan, its most famous member.

In the 1920s, it was the turn of anglo poets to group together in the McGill Movement which introduced the principles of literary modernism to Canada (members included A.J.M. Smith, F.R. Scott, John Glassco, A.M. Klein and Leo Kennedy).

In an essay on the development of fiction in English Montreal in the now-defunct literary magazine *Rubicon*, Hugh Hood refers to "some cyclical pattern of recurrence woven into the genetic structure of this city which makes it easy prey to epidemic outbursts of poetry... or fiction... as much in English as in the language of the large French-speaking majority of the population, at intervals of about twenty years."

The city's literary pulse quickened once more in the 1940s. Gratien Gélinas was then writing and performing his Fridolin skits to enormous popular success. Mavis Gallant, in her twenties ("living like a bird on a branch, from twig to twig"), subsisted by writing radio columns for the old *Montreal Standard* while publishing her first short stories in the little magazine *Preview*. Poets Louis Dudek (that "tall thin drink of water" in the words of fellow poet Raymond Souster), F.R. Scott, et al, congregated at Irving Layton's Côte St. Luc home on Kildare Road, then surrounded by open fields, to read their works and play a parlour game called Poetry Poker. A.M. Klein had just published his *Rocking Chair* (1944) collection and Hugh MacLennan and Gabrielle Roy would publish *Two Solitudes* and *Bonheur d'occasion* in 1945.

In English-language poetry, the cycle was particularly high in the 1940s and 1950s, Montreal leading Canada in a "spring cleaning of Victorian dust and cobwebs, in the renovation that is called modernism," in the words of Louis Dudek. P.K. Page, Miriam

Waddington, Layton, Dudek, and editor John Sutherland participated, amongst others, in an extraordinary outburst of energy that
gave birth to little magazines, bohemian lifestyles and fierce and passionate poems imbued with a sense of mission and relevance.

In the late 1950s and 1960s, Leonard Cohen emerged as a startling voice: the award-winning poet and novelist metamorphosed
into enigmatic balladeer and international celebrity.

Meanwhile, the Quiet Revolution and its not-so-quiet ramifica-
tions were catalyzing and being catalyzed by literary activity in French
Montreal. The 1960s saw the emergence of Wunderkinder Marie-
Claire Blais, Réjean Ducharme and Michel Tremblay whose works
have powerfully influenced readers and writers over the last thirty
years.

Few Montreal literary movements have had a more profound
impact than the one launched by the short-lived and seemingly-mar-
ginal literary journal *Parti pris* (1963-68). Founded soon after the
first wave of FLQ bombings, *Parti pris* advocated a sovereign and
socialist Quebec and consisted mainly of budding writers in their
twenties such as Paul Chamberland, André Major and Jacques
Renaud, and with Jacques Ferron, one of Quebec's greatest short
story writers (and a novelist, physician and founder of the satirical
Rhinoceros party) as unofficial father figure.

In 1965 a special issue of *Parti pris* entitled "Pour une littérature
québécoise" first proposed the label "québécoise" to describe a literature that had so far been known as "canadienne française". Soon
the self-concept of a whole people was implicated, and many French-
speaking Quebecers began to think of themselves as Québécois.

At about the same time, the success of Michel Tremblay's daz-
zling play, *Les Belles-soeurs*, in 1968 added fuel to the fire of the controversy raging over the literary use of *joual*, the juicy proletarian
dialect of Quebec. *Joual* (a corruption of the word cheval) would
provide inspiration for the songs of Robert Charlebois and give rise
to an important body of works in the theatre and cinema, although—
with the exception of a few writers such as Victor-Lévy Beaulieu
and Tremblay himself—it has fallen by the wayside in the novel.

In the 1970s, the most notable development on the local literary
scene was what critic Ben-Z. Shek has called "the emergence of the

feminist 'I'." Innovative and audacious, the feminist school has created its own magazines and drama companies, treated the female body and lesbianism openly and developed a literary movement which challenges conventional language structures and genres as "patriarchal." The formal inventiveness of Nicole Brossard, France Théoret and Jovette Marchessault to name only a few of the French practitioners, finds parallels on the English side in the award-winning poetry of Erin Mouré and the prose of Gail Scott.

Scott has written, "I concur completely with Nicole Brossard's statement that 'Writing I am a woman is full of consequences.' Questions like aesthetics, ideology, time, space are intricate elements of the language exploration process that is part of our emergence from centuries of oppressive patriarchal culture. We need new forms, new syntax, new cities, even, where we can live, speak, as whole, integral women."

Also in the 1970s, two English literary movements expressed other realities of "montréalitude"—to borrow a term coined by Clark Blaise. In prose, then youthful literati John Metcalf, Ray Smith, Ray Fraser, Blaise and Hugh Hood banded together—"a jolly band of prose-troubadours"—to form the original Montreal Story Tellers. In search of dollars and an audience, they read their works in Montreal English-language high schools, colleges and universities and talked insistently about being Canadian writers at a time when— as John Metcalf has written— "to read Canadian matter and talk of Canadian concerns was ... like carrying the Word to people who ate grubs and worshipped aeroplanes."

Simultaneously, a group of young poets associated with an innovative series of poetry readings at the artist-run Véhicule Art gallery began to challenge the conservative and academic mindset which had once again beset the English-language poetry scene. New Delta, successor to Delta Canada founded by Louis Dudek and others in 1963, began publishing Bob McGee, Richard Sommer, Michael Harris, and Robert Allen. Experimenting with "form, content and collectivity," Ken Norris, Artie Gold, Stephen Morrissey, Claudia Lapp, John McAuley, Tom Konyves, and Endre Farkas, were published by Maker Press and Véhicule Press. In the coming decade, other poets came to be associated with Véhicule Press which was founded in 1973 as an offshoot of the gallery: Peter Van Toorn, Raymond Filip, Ann Diamond, Robyn Sarah, Michael Harris, David Solway—and the list goes on! Distinguished by a diversity of styles and influences, they represented the local literary coming-of-age of the baby boom generation.

The 1980s saw the impact of a melange of diverse influences. Of significance on the French side was the advent of the commercially successful Québécois blockbuster novel exemplified by Yves Beauchem in's *Le Matou* (*The Alleycat*, which was translated into fifteen languages and sold 1,200,000 copies) and Arlette Cousture's *Les Filles du Caleb* (Émilie, the turn-of-the-century love story based on the life of Cousture's grandmother. It sold nearly half a million copies and, as a television series, set records for its viewing audience).

At the same time, new and cosmopolitan voices had begun to be heard in French. For instance, irreverent sexual satirist Dany Laferrière, physician Joel Des Rosiers (who in his spare time writes poetry that has been nominated for a Governor-General's Award) and Université de Montréal literature professor Émile Ollivier (whose novel *Passages* about flight from Haiti won the 1992 Prix de Montréal) are only the most prominent members of a community of writers from Haiti relocated in Montreal (Laferrière now spends most of his time in Miami but still publishes here).

In the late 1980s and currently, in the 1990s, English Montreal appears to be undergoing one of its periodic literary booms. Novels and short-story collections by Will Aitken, Ann Diamond, Trevor Ferguson, David Homel, P. Scott Lawrence, Linda Leith, Yann Martel, Edward O.Phillips, Kenneth Radu, T.F. Rigelhof, Gail Scott, Ray Smith, and Sharon Sparling attest to the healthy state of English-language letters. One should also at least mention the fine non-fiction work being written by, among other Montrealers, Louise Abbott, Charles Foran, John Goddard, Mary Meigs, Witold Rybczynski, David Solway, Charles Taylor and Ruth Wisse.

Doubtless, the founding in 1987 of the Quebec Society for the Promotion of English-Language Literature—QSPELL—has been instrumental in raising the profile of English-language writers by awarding prizes for distinguished poetry, fiction and non-fiction.

(In 1991-92 there were fifty-two eligible entries written by English-language Quebec residents in English submitted to QSPELL.) But writers of distinction have been honing their talent here for a long time; the awards acknowledge ability, they don't create it.

Stepping back from the literary fray, one would have to agree with Ann Charney who, in 1991, wrote in *Books in Canada* that "to be a writer in Quebec is to live life on the schizoid edge of cultural dissociation." She cited two literary events held on the same day in the fall of 1990. A couple of blocks apart, memorials were being observed for Hugh MacLennan and Alice Parizeau, each an eminent member of their respective literary communities. "The two events might as well (have been) continents and centuries apart for all the cognizance they (took) of each other."

While researching *The Writers of Montreal*, I criss-crossed over this cultural divide, first in my reading and then, for several exhilarating weeks in the late winter and spring of 1993, face to face with many of the authors. Whether for the insights they gave me of the writing process (the ebullient Irving Layton compared poetic inspiration to "a series of cerebral orgasms"), or the light they shed upon the writers' own personalities (Yves Beauchemin told me that, were he in my shoes, he, too, would view his brand of Québécois nationalism as narrow), these meetings led me to hope that, in some modest way, this book might help bridge the solitudes for which this city is notorious.

In this aspiration, I stand in good company. Nicole Brossard praised the project for "reminding us of all our great writers." Jovette Marchessault expressed her frustration that, though she had described in umpteen interviews her indebtedness to Montreal's anglophone Jewish community (whose support had originally enabled her to establish herself as an artist), her gratitude had never been reported.

But it was Marie-Claire Blais who put it most feelingly.

At the end of our interview, the renowned novelist signed her latest book, *L'Exilé*, for me with the words, "in hopes that our two cultures will join in art and literature."

PART ONE

From Cartier's Hochelaga to MacLennan's *Two Solitudes*

Montreal ca. 1851. Craig Street near Beaver Hall Hill.
Daguerreotype, National Archives of Canada

Writing About Montreal Began Even Before the City Was Born

VISUALIZE A THOUSAND NATIVE INDIANS in festive mood mobbing the shoreline of Montreal when the city was as yet less than a gleam in the eye of history.

"Making great signs of joy," the Indians of Hochelaga ("beaver dams" in Huron) greeted Jacques Cartier and his band of sailors and gentlemen adventurers with exuberant hospitality "for the men danced in one ring, the women in another and the children also apart by themselves. After this they brought us quantities of fish, and of their bread which is made of Indian corn, throwing so much of it into our longboats that it seemed to rain bread."

With this extraordinary mutual sighting of native and European, Montreal made its literary debut in the *The Voyages of Jacques Cartier*, 107 years before the city's official founding in 1642. Most historians believe that the terse, third-person narrative was taken from a ship's log kept by Cartier, a Breton seaman, but ghost-written by someone else, possibly François Rabelais, the great sixteenth-century French humanist and satirist.

Cartier's *Voyages* is but one of several early narratives and memoirs that detail Montreal's beginnings.

During the French régime, churchmen and women with little thought to either publication or posterity recorded both the dramatic and mundane events unfolding around them for the benefit of their counterparts in the mother country.

The city's first official historian, François Dollier de Casson, undertook to set down in writing the pioneering settlement's first three decades though he himself had only been here a couple of years at the time, in 1672.

Soldier, priest, missionary, explorer, city planner and architect, Dollier made an able amateur historian. In fact, much of what we know about the original founders of Montreal—Maisonneuve, Jeanne Mance, Marguerite Bourgeoys, chief among them—and their zeal to establish the religious utopia that was Montreal's original *raison d'être* is derived from him.

By all accounts, he was a pretty interesting character himself. Of huge stature and with strength enough to lift two men at a time— one in each hand, so it was said—he did not hesitate to throw his weight around. (While kneeling at his prayers, he was once interrupted by a young Indian who dared to mock him. Dollier remained on his knees but with one shot of his arm sent the younger man sprawling.)

After considerable missionary activity in the Great Lakes and Mississippi regions (he laid official claim to Lake Ontario for France), Dollier was named Superior of the Sulpicians and became seigneur of Montreal. He laid out the city's first streets and designed the Sulpician Seminary, Montreal's oldest building, which still stands on Notre Dame Street at Place d'Armes.

Dollier's *Histoire de Montréal* combined oral history with his own eye-witness observations. He drew heavily on the memories of Jeanne Mance, Mountreal's co-founder with Maisonneuve, for the period before his own arrival to the colony.

The idea of Providence as the moving force of history loomed large in Dollier's world view. He attributed the reason for Maisonneuveuve's coming to these "very remote countries" as simply "The time having arrived when Providence wanted to employ him upon its work."

But as well as moralizing, Dollier could tell a good, racy story. There's the one, for instance, about three Iroquois who ambushed "goodwife Primot" in 1652 and "threw themselves upon her to kill her with their hatchets. At this the woman defended herself like a lioness, but as she had no weapons but hands and feet, at the third or fourth blow they felled her as if dead. Immediately one of the Iroquois flung himself upon her to scalp her and escape with this shameful trophy. But as our amazon felt herself so seized, she at once recovered her senses, raised herself, and more fierce than ever, caught hold of this monster so forcibly by a place which modesty forbids us to mention that he could not free himself."

In less than a generation, Montreal was transformed from an austere mission station to the colony's principal fur trade emporium, doing a roaring business in skins, booze and women. But, as the *Jesuit Relations* reveal, Montrealers cavorted at their wildest on New France's western borders.

A marvellous compendium of texts, the *Relations* is the collective name of a series of reports sent by New France Jesuits to their Superior in Paris. The collection includes letters, reports and journals of priests and missionaries both from the main colony and from more widespread outposts in North America.

For many years a missionary to the Cayuga Iroquois (who did not take kindly to proselytization), Étienne de Carheil was reassigned to a mission among the Hurons at Michilimackinac in present-day Michigan in 1686. Here he fought relentslessly against the brandy trade with the Indians, which did not endear him to the coureurs de bois from Montreal against whom he railed bitterly for their "lewd and shameless conduct."

In a letter to the Governor of Quebec in 1702 from Michilimackinac, de Carheil complained of "the most scandalous Evil of all... I refer to single women, women without husbands, women who are mistresses of their own Bodies, women who can dispose of them to these men, and whom the latter know to be willing to do so,—in a word, They are the prostitutes of Montreal, who are alternately brought here and taken back..."

The fur traders defended their choice of women employees with some canny arguments that resonate in the contemporary ear: clearly the issue of Canadian women's wage inequity has deep roots.

"The pretext that they usually allege for taking women in preference to men," Father de Carheil wrote, "is that women cost them less than men, and are satisfied with lower wages. They speak the truth; but the very fact of their being Satisfied with less wages is a manifest proof of their dissoluteness. If they Were wise would they not ask to be paid the same as men, since they perform the same services—and frequently do more, by Cutting wood for them and by Cooking their food, which men will not do?"

A prototype of the stalwart pioneering woman New France is renowned for, Marie Morin contrasted starkly with the women de Carheil condemned. The first Canadian-born nun, Morin can also be called our first homegrown historian, if the concept of history is stretched to include annals of a narrow variety.

She was born in Quebec in 1649, into a family of twelve children. As a ten-year-old boarder at the Ursulines in Quebec, the little girl formed a passionate desire to come to Montreal to be a nurse after a visit by Jeanne Mance and three nursing nuns who had been chosen to found the Hôtel-Dieu Hospital of Ville Marie.

With the Iroquois steadily pounding away at them, Montrealers clearly needed a hospital. Marie's parents, however, wouldn't hear of sending her off to the perils of the frontier when she could join a safe nursing order in Quebec. Thirteen-year-old Marie prevailed by convincing Bishop Laval himself to issue her a special authorization.

After she took her vows, she proved a capable leader and businesswoman, elected alternately financial manager and Mother Superior of her order over many terms.

Her memoirs, *Les Annales de l'Hôtel Dieu de Montréal, 1659-1725*, are written in a blunt style and with extravagant orthography for which she apologized in the preface, citing her many responsibilities for the overseeing of the building's construction and reconstruction after two serious fires. "The carpenters, masons, stone-cutters, and joiners needed to speak to me often, and that distracted me from my subject and caused me to make untimely repetitions and cut too short an account I had already begun."

She writes of the city's early founders, of English attacks, of the looters during two fires who sampled the hospital's strong medicines, and even of a personal visit by the devil.

Of special interest is her attention to domestic detail. Morin's description of Canadian winters before the advent of central heating is particulary chilling.

"You must know that the cold in this country can be understood only by those who are subjected to it. Their houses having holes in more than 200 places, the wind and snow easily passed through them ... so that when there had been wind and snow during the night, one of the first things to be done in the morning was to take wooden shovels and the broom to throw out the snow around the doors and windows ... and the water that was put on the table for drinking froze within a quarter of an hour."

Imbued with religious idealism, the church mothers and fathers succeeded in reconciling for themselves Providence's finger and the harshness of the situation in which they found themselves. Without a jot of literary pretensiousness, they made excellent if rough-hewn reporters. Their accounts are delightfully unselfconscious and surprisingly lively.

L'HISTORIEN MICHEL BIBAUD.

MICHEL BIBAUD

Curmudgeonly Littérateur

JOURNALIST, POET, HISTORIAN AND EDITOR, Michel Bibaud was a jack of all literary trades and a master of none. Yet he has earned a niche in Montreal's literary history by achieving a couple of "firsts": he was both the first French Canadian to publish a collection of poetry and the first to write a history of Canada.

Bibaud was born in 1782 at what is now 4505 Côte-des-Neiges (the site is marked by a commemorative plaque), one of nine children of a poor farming family. He was almost nineteen (the customary age of graduation from classical college) when he entered Montreal's College Saint-Raphael, probably due to his family's straitened circumstances. Rather than pursuing studies in the liberal professions as wealthier young men did, he began working as a teacher immediately upon graduation.

Soon he added journalism to his repertoire, and then combined writing with teaching by bringing out a mathematics textbook. With a large family to support, Bibaud embarked on one journalistic venture after another. He founded *L'Aurore*, a political, scientific and literary weekly, in 1817, and became the editor of *Le Spectateur canadien* when *L'Aurore* merged with it in 1819.

Bibaud's most significant literary venture was the launching of *La Bibliothèque canadienne*, a cultural and scientific monthly, in 1825. Like a number of other periodicals with which he came to be associated, it used local talent almost exclusively and was dedicated to the advancement of French Canadians.

A prodigious if plodding worker, Bibaud's strongly didactic bent, notoriously disagreeable nature and unpopular political views did much to alienate his contemporaries. *Épîtres, satires, chansons, épigrammes, et autres pièces de vers,* his historic poetry anthology which appeared in 1830, for instance, contained four lengthy "satires" condemning French Canadians in turn for avarice, envy, sloth and ignorance. The poems dripped with heavy-handed irony and were almost totally devoid of humor. The twentieth-century critic Séraphin Marion characterized his style as that of "a lumberjack putting up his cottage."

Bibaud's two-volume history—*Histoire du Canada, sous la domination française* (1837), and *Histoire du Canada, et des Canadiens, sous la domination anglaise*(1844)—falls well short both in scope and scholarship of the *Histoire du Canada* published a few years later by his brilliant Quebec-city contemporary, Francois-Xavier Garneau.

Curmudgeonly and opinionated, Bibaud had the courage to go against the prevailing political tide. While he devoted his whole career towards raising the cultural consciousness of his people and was imbued with a strong sense of national pride, he denounced the 1837 revolutionaries and pronounced in favour of British institutions like the monarchy and responsible government. In a strongly nationalistic period, this won him few friends.

Despite his shortcomings, Bibaud made an important contribution to French-Canadian culture as the editor of *La Bibiliothèque canadienne* and similar periodicals which encouraged the development of a homegrown literature. In 1856 he suffered a stroke and died a year later.

The following is an 1823 poem by Michel Bibaud defending the use of French in Quebec. "Simon" is a fictional English-language journalist; "Guillaume" is William the Conqueror. The poem appeared in *Épîtres, satires, chansons, épigrammes, et autres pièces de vers* (Montreal: L. Duvernay, 1830).

Tu perds l'esprit, ou plutôt la raison
Ou je n'air rien compris à ta harangue:
Y penses-tu, mon compère Simon,

De comparer le coeur avec la langue?
On baille un coeur, mais une langue, non:
Je ne crois pas même que l'on en change
Comme d'habit, ou bien d'affection;
Et ta leçon me semble assez étrange,
Et puis donnée assez mal à propos;
Me souvenant qu'en dépit d'un héros,
(Je veux parler de ce bon roi Guillaume,)
Maître absolu dans son nouveau royaume,
Tout les Anglais parlent encore anglais:
(J'entends ici les Anglais d'Angleterre.)
Moi, sans craindre le procès,
Je veux parler le français,
Langue de mes père et mère;
Et la raison à le faire
Me porte par maint endroit:
Mais, surtout, je veux comprendre
Ces grands mots: Dieu et Mon Droit,
Que tout Anglais doit entendre,
Et que plus d'un n'entend pas.
Que si quelqu'un s'en offense,
Je réponds, sans embarras:
Honni soit qui mal y pense.

D.-B. VIGER

Le père
de la presse Canadienne

A WEEK BEFORE CHRISTMAS in 1838, Denis-Benjamin Viger, hoary-headed with age at sixty-four, was refused his freedom from prison unless he posted bail for future good conduct.

Politician, lawyer, constitutional expert, landed proprietor, Viger (1774-1861) had been second only to his cousin, Louis-Joseph Papineau, as a leader of the 1837 Rebellion in Lower Canada. The old man refused to post bail because, he reasoned, to do so would be to imply that his previous conduct had been wrong.

The price of his high principles was nineteen months in jail. He was not allowed to see anyone. He could not have paper, pen, or newspapers.

Newspapers were what had singled Viger out from other revolutionaries for the severity of his punishment in the first place. The papers he owned or controlled in 1837-38—*La Minerve, La Quotidienne* and *Le Temps*—were accused (justly) of spreading discontent and diffusing ideas concerning independence for French Canada during "the troubles."

Over his long career, Viger was involved with many papers. His first published piece had appeared in Fleury Mesplet's *Gazette de Montréal*, a bilingual newspaper in 1792, when Viger was only eighteen. He also financed the nationalist *L'Aurore* and *L'Ordre*, a Catholic and establishment-oriented organ in the 1850s. His involvement with the press has earned him the title of "le père de la presse canadienne."

Newspapers filled a role, among others, in colonial Canada that today is the preserve of *Hansard*. Until 1867, newspapers, along with their general mandate of supplying news, also shouldered the job of comprehensive reporting of the debates in the Legislative Assembly.

And Canada's deeply political colonial population not only expected to read the speeches of parliamentarians, they expected the coverage in papers which represented their own specific political views and interests. This resulted in an astonishing array of newspapers in a small province. In 1836 twenty papers flourished in Lower Canada.

By 1871 Montreal alone supported sixteen papers. Two publishers, Honoré Beaugrand and Alphonse Desjardins, became mayors of the city in the late nineteenth century, a fact that attests to the prestige with which the public regarded the profession.

But to return to Viger. Universally respected when he emerged from jail—even his cousin Papineau always referred to him as "Monsieur" and he was generally called "le Vénérable"—within three years he was to fall ignominiously from grace. During one of the last crises before the obtaining of responsible government, Viger made a stunning error in judgement. He sided with Lord Metcalfe, a governor who was sympathetic to the aspirations of French Canadians but who nevertheless insisted on governing in his own name, refusing to bow to the demands for majority, party rule. Viger, who accepted the co-premiership in Lord Metcalfe's administration, became in the view of the *Canadiens*, a *vendu*, a sellout.

It was a sincere, if misguided, performance by one of the most distinguished actors on the Canadian political and cultural stage of the first half of the nineteenth century. (His role encited at least as much controversy and commentary in the press of his time as did that of Parti-Québécois-luminary Claude Morin when his freelancing for the RCMP came to light in recent days.) In the end, the *Montreal Gazette*—a paper that had often judged Viger severely—observed that the justification for his actions was to be found in "a desire to secure the blessings of free government for his fellow countrymen."

Though a fixture in politics from the 1790s, Viger was not a good orator. ("Long of nose and long of speech," his critics charged after one of his droning performances in the Assembly.) A prolific writer of constitutional treatises and opinion pieces for the press, his prose style was also long winded and convoluted in the extreme.

Yet he was one of the most cultivated men of his time. His library contained over 3,000 volumes, he had one of the best art collections in the colony and probably its richest wine cellar. He lived to be eighty-six, fortunate to die a peaceful death, unlike his wife who had suffered the ravages of cholera seven years before him.

Extract from a letter by D.B. Viger, quoted in *La Vie studieuse et obstinée de Denis-Benjamin Viger*, by Gérard Parizeau (Montreal: Fides, 1980), 185-186.

Viger wrote the letter to Lord Stanley, Secretary of State for the Colonies, in 1833 during a stay in London while serving as agent for Lower Canada. Written in English, the letter is about the extent of the governor's responsibilities for the actions of his subordinates.

... in England the King's person is inviolable. He is not responsible for the faults or errors of his servents (sic). When they are of a nature to produce such complaints, he is not precipitated from the throne, in the expectation that they will be hushed, at the same time retaining in office those, who by the advice which he was bound to follow have let (sic) him astray. Even admitting that such means were adopted to restore harmony, his successor would not doubtless be compelled to be surrounded by the same men, to submit to the same advice, to persue (sic) the same cause of conduct... And that is really what exists in Canada. He who holds the range (sic) of government is responsible for his errors, and so it should be; but he is in front of fact the only one. Those who lead him astray are invested with that degree of invariability which is only attached to the King's person.

ROMAN CANADIEN

PAR

MADAME LEPROHON

ANTOINETTE

DE

MIRECOURT

Traduit de l'anglais par

J. A. GENAND

MONTRÉAL

C. O. BEAUCHEMIN ET VALOIS, ÉDITEURS,

RUE ST. PAUL, 237 et 239.

1865

ROSANNA LEPROHON

Bridging Montreal's Dualities with Finesse

THE FIRST CANADIAN NOVEL was not written by a Canadian. Published in London in 1769 and written by Frances Brooke, an Englishwoman who had just returned from five years with the British garrison at Quebec City where her husband was chaplain, *The History of Emily Montague* took as its setting and subject the world of French Canada after the Conquest. In the novel, Brooke set in motion all the social elements of eighteenth-century Quebec—British soldiers, *Canadien* peasants, high society French, Indians—against the natural backdrop of the New World.

One hundred years later, Montreal novelist Rosanna Mullins Leprohon (1829-79) dealt with the same subject matter and many of the same themes as Brooke. But what is curious and fascinating about Leprohon is that though she wrote in English, her literary reputation and renown were much greater in French. Her most popular work, *The Manor House of de Villerai*, was originally published in serial form in English by the *Montreal Family Herald* in 1859-60. But in French translation, it went through six different editions as late as 1925.

The daughter of Irish immigrants, Rosanna was already publishing flowery, genteel prose and verse at seventeen, even before completing her studies at the Congregation of Notre-Dame, a convent which offered schooling and moral instruction to the daughters of

Montreal's wealthy citizens.

When her first poems appeared in *The Literary Garland*—the most successful of a crop of Montreal-based early Canadian literary magazines—Susanna Moodie hailed her as "one of the gifted, upon whom fancy smiled in her cradle, and genius marked ... for his own."

Five years later, in 1851, Rosanna married Dr. Jean-Lukin Leprohon, a descendant of an old French-Canadian family, and settled for a time in St. Charles-sur-Richelieu. Domesticity and motherhood initially stalled her creativity. (She gave birth to thirteen children, five of whom, including her first, died in infancy.) But ultimately her marriage proved invaluable to her literary career. Through her husband and his family she came to have intimate knowledge of upper-class French-Canadian society, and her stay in the Richelieu area gave her an understanding of the aspirations and values of French-Canadian nationalists.

These strands of knowledge and sympathy would subsequently inform her fiction when she returned to Montreal and resumed writing once more in earnest.

Three of her most significant novels appeared in the 1860s. All three, *The Manor House of DeVillerai*, *Antoinette de Mirecourt* and *Armand Durand*, were translated into French and serialized in magazines in both languages.

Like many Irish-Catholic Montrealers, Leprohon bridged French and English dualities with finesse. Her language of composition was English, but she was perfectly bilingual and chose French Canadians as her main characters. Her favourite period was the one Frances Brooke had written of as a contemporary: just "after the royal standard of England had replaced the fleurs-de-lys of France."

While Brooke was a superior artist, critics have praised Leprohon's novels as more authentic in detail and atmosphere. Her novels, though stilted, melodramatic and conventional, also carry some sophisticated themes. Her own marriage seems to have given her psychological insight into the difficulties of loving another of different background, temperament and social class.

She was also a strong Canadian nationalist and an early champion of Canadian literature. "Although the literary treasures of 'the old world' are ever open to us, and our American neighbours should continue to inundate the country with reading-matter, intended to meet all wants and suit all tastes and sympathies, at prices which enable every one to partake of this never-failing and ever-varying feast; yet Canadians should not be discouraged from endeavouring to form and foster a literature of their own," she wrote in the preface to *Antoinette de Mirecourt*. Then she added modestly that if her novel "possesses no other merit, it will, at least, be found to have that of being essentially Canadian."

In fact, as the first Canadian writer to be widely read in both English and French, Leprohon stands in the company of Gabrielle Roy and Hugh MacLennan. Her talent falls far short of theirs, but she deserves more recognition than she has so far received.

An excerpt from *Antoinette de Mirecourt; or Secret Marrying and Secret Sorrowing* by Rosanna Leprohon (Montreal: Lovell, 1864; Toronto: McClelland & Stewart, New Canadian Library, 1973), 19-20.

CHAPTER 1

The feeble sun of November, that most unpleasant month in our Canadian year, was streaming down on the narrow streets and irregular buildings of Montreal, such as it existed in the year 176-...

Reflecting back the red sunlight in the countless small panes of its narrow casements, stood a large and substantial-looking stone house, situated towards the east extremity of Notre Dame street, then the aristocratic quarter of the city... Despite the lowness of the ceilings..., despite the rough wood-carving..., there is a stamp of unmistakable wealth and refinement pervading the abode.

Glimpses of fine old paintings, costly inlaid cabinets, antique vases ... confirm this impression...

The master of the house, a plain-featured but gentlemanly-looking man, was seated, at the moment in which we introduce him to the reader, in his large and well-lighted library... when the door of the apartment opened, and an elegant looking woman, on the shady side of Balzac's admired feminine age of thirty, and dressed with the most exquisite taste and care, entered.

THOMAS D'ARCY McGEE

Son of Ireland,
Father of Confederation

BURIED IN MONTREAL on his forty-third birthday after an assassin's bullet had felled him in Ottawa, Thomas D'Arcy McGee (1825-1868) packed several lifetimes into his one short one.

He arrived in Montreal in 1857 and spent only a quarter of his life in Cananda, yet his funeral was the biggest the city had ever seen. Six grey horses pulled the glass-panelled bier over which hung a black cloth decorated with a silver harp and a shamrock. Thousands crowded the streets and overflowed the two services held in his honour at St. Patrick's and Notre Dame churches.

McGee figures in the pages of Canadian history primarily as an ardent proponent of Confederation. But while he played an active part in politics, he mainly earned his living as a journalist, author and lecturer.

His mercurial career embraced two continents, four countries and a multitude of causes frequently at war with one another. Before he ever came to Canada, he had been a newspaper reporter and publisher in Boston, London, Dublin and New York. He was also a brilliant orator. Even sharing the political stage with such noted public speakers as John A. Macdonald, George-Étienne Cartier and George Brown, McGee was the acknowledged king.

He had arrived in Boston from Ireland in 1842, at the age of seventeen, and had galvanized an audience with an impromptu speech days after his arrival. One of his listeners commented, "I wish to God … that such little curly-headed Paddies as that would come to us by whole shiploads; any country may feel proud of that youth." The next day he was offered a job at the *Boston Pilot* newspaper.

McGee's deeply-felt connections to Irish history, literature and culture were the constants in his firmament, but his repeated about-faces of opinion laid him open to charges of opportunism. At different times in his life he denounced the Catholic Church and clergy, subsequently to affirm his deep faith in Catholicism. Towards the beginning and end of his life, he espoused temperance; in between he was a heavy drinker.

Back in Ireland in his early twenties, he helped to found the revolutionary Young Ireland party and participated in an unsuccessful revolt against England in 1848. Twenty years later he became the most vocal opponent of the Fenians—the heirs to Young Ireland—and was in fact assassinated by a Fenian sympathizer. An underlying irony heightened the tragedy, for McGee was a renowned conciliator: in all of Canada he was regarded as a genius at compromise.

A prolific writer of poetry and prose, at eighteen McGee wrote a historical novel and in the 1860s a drama intended for students in Catholic schools. All his other prose work was historical, most of it propaganda to justify a position through historical rationalization. His best work is thought to be *A Popular History of Ireland* (1863) which won him election to the Royal Irish Academy.

As a writer of lyrical, romantic poetry and of historical ballads, McGee was celebrated in Ireland as among the finest verse-writers of his age. Some of his poetry remains touching even today; some of it is quite dreadful. (The poem "Jacques Cartier" begins "In the sea-port of Saint Malo, 'twas a smiling morn, in May/When the Commodore Jacques Cartier to the westward sail'd away.")

But his collected speeches (from which an excerpt is reproduced below) still leap boldly from the fusty pages of yellowing texts. Even without the impassioned oratorical style for which he was famous, the measured phrases and noble sentiments capture the reader.

Many of McGee's ideas have a truly modern ring. He called, for instance, for the establishment of a separate province with extensive economic assistance for native people. He believed fervently in the development of a distinctly Canadian literature, and proposed tariff protection for Canadian publishers.

For sheer charisma and brilliant achievement in the eleven years he spent in Canada, McGee remains unsurpassed. Just before his death in 1868, he had expressed a desire to leave politics; he intended to turn his full attention to Canadian history and literature. The assassin's bullet cheated him, and us, of much.

An extract of a speech, "The Policy of Conciliation," made by Thomas D'Arcy McGee in Montreal, March 1861 "in reply to the toast of his health, at a dinner given him by his constituents," from *1825-D'Arcy McGee-1925; A Collection of Speeches and Addresses*, edited by Charles Murphy (Toronto: Macmillan, 1937), 165-167.

… there is nothing to be more dreaded in this country than feuds arising from exaggerated feelings of religion and nationality. On the other hand, the one thing needed for making Canada the happiest of homes, is to rub down all sharp angles, and to remove all those asperities which divide our people on questions of origin and religious profession…

In Canada, with men of all origins and all kinds of culture, if we do not bear and forbear, if we do not get rid of old quarrels, but on the contrary make fresh ones, … then, Gentlemen, we shall return to what Hobbes considered the state of Nature—I mean the state of war…

I know, and you know, that I can never cease to regard with an affection which amounts to idolatry, the land where I spent my best, my first years, where I obtained the partner of my life, and where my firstborn saw the light. I cannot but regard that land even with increased love because she has not been prosperous. Yet I hold we have no right to intrude our Irish patriotism on this soil; for our first duty is to the land where we live and have fixed our homes, and where, while we live, we must find the true sphere of our duties…

LOUIS FRÉCHETTE

Unofficial Poet Laureate of Quebec

AS A LITTLE BOY growing up in the 1840s in Lévis across the St. Lawrence from Quebec City, Louis Fréchette (1839-1908) played street games in which he invoked the name of Louis-Joseph Papineau, the leader of the 1837-38 Rebellions in Lower Canada. And, as he wrote in his memoirs a half century later, he would gaze across the river toward the Plains of Abraham where "dominating the high mounds, there loomed in the distance the rounded stumps of heavy Martello towers, advanced sentinels of the haughty citadel of Quebec encircled by cannons, where the English flag waved."

The little boy who would try to explain to himself why that flag hung there when "nous étions français, nous! Nous parlions français, nos livres étaient français..." grew up to become the principal literary figure of French-speaking Canada, its unofficial poet laureate, the only nineteenth-century French-Canadian writer to be well-known outside Canada.

His move to Montreal in 1877 from Quebec City also signalled Montreal's newly-assumed status as literary and cultural capital of the province.

In a life that included a stint in the proverbial garret and was capped by the Montyon Prize of the Académie Française, Fréchette was, for more than a quarter of a century, the symbol of the ideal man of letters: a poet who had penned over 400 verses, a playwright, essayist, folklorist and short story writer.

Radical in his politics, he was also constantly embroiled in polemics, and something of a fraud.

The second half of his career was dogged by frequently validated charges of plagiarism. A symbolic precursor of this charge, and one for which Fréchette was not to blame, was his play, *Félix Poutré*. A popular historical drama based on the memoirs of one Félix Poutré who claimed to have been a leader of the 1837-38 Rebellions, its hero later turned out to be a paid informer working for the military police against the Patriotes.

Critics of his day acclaimed Fréchette as "the Lamartine of Canada," evoking the name of the great French Romantic poet and revolutionary politician. His first collections were alternately romantically, then politically inspired. Many of his early lyrical verses were sparked by amorous adventures and bore titles such as "Corinne" and "Juliette." His second book, *La Voix d'un exilé*, was written in Chicago where he exiled himself in 1866 in disgust over the approach of Confederation, which he deemed would end the future of the French-Canadian nation.

La Voix d'un exilé was used as propaganda by the Rouge party in Canada. One twentieth-century critic has called its "violence of … language" unsurpassed in Canadian literature. (A typically incendiary poem implied that Thomas D'Arcy McGee had met his end by assassination for his betrayal of the Irish people.) According to what may be an apocryphal account, when Fréchette became the province's establishment poet in 1880, he bought up all the copies of *La Voix* he could find and burned them.

A lawyer by profession, Fréchette made a stab at politics when he returned to Canada from Chicago in 1871. He sat in the House of Commons for four years but failed to get re-elected.

His marriage at age thirty-eight to a Montreal heiress in 1876 changed the course of his life. While he continued to have strong political opinions (his anti-clericalism, in particular, was very controversial in his time), he no longer needed to worry about his financial future and could write full time.

Ensconced in a mansion in St. Louis Square, he wrote *Les Fleurs boréales*, the collection that won him the Montyon prize and assured his reputation. He may have been the first (but would certainly not be the last) Canadian for whom fame abroad meant recognition at home.

La Légende d'un peuple, a series of historical tableaux interpreting the emergence of the French-Canadian nation, was published in 1887 and is regarded as Fréchette's finest work. This collection of epic poems reminiscent of Victor Hugo reflects the cult of great men popular in the nineteenth century. Several poems take as their subjects heroes of French Canada such as Dollard des Ormeaux, Jolliet and Papineau.

When Fréchette died some twenty years later, few people attended his funeral. Tastes had changed, romanticism was becoming passé, new literary movements frowned on his imitative talent. Yet Fréchette at his best could rise above his own mediocrity. His description of the immense Mississippi, for instance, in the long poem "Jolliet" still stirs the imagination, still plucks at the heart.

From "Jolliet" in *La Légende d'un peuple* by Louis Fréchette: Poésies choisies, Volume I (Montreal: Beauchemin, 1908), 99-100.

> Le grand fleuve dormait couché dans la savane.
> Dans les lointains brumeux passaient en caravane
> De farouches troupeaux d'élans et de bisons.
> Drapé dans les rayons de l'aube matinale,
> Le désert déployait sa splendeur virginale
>   Sur d'insondables horizons.
>
> Juin brillait. Sur les eaux, dans l'herbe des pelouses,
> Sur les sommets, au fond des profondeurs jalouses,
> L'Été fécond chantait ses sauvages amours.
> Du Sud à l'Aquilon, du Couchant à l'Aurore,
> Toute l'immensité semblait garder encore
>   La majesté des premiers jours…

ÉMILE NELLIGAN

Triumph and Tragedy

HE LOOKED LIKE A GREEK GOD, wrote like an angel and succumbed to
madness before reaching the age of twenty. The meteoric talent and
tormented destiny of Émile Nelligan (1879-1941) have long trans-
fixed French Canada. His life has inspired an opera and a ballet, a
prestigious poetry prize bears his name and his writings have gener-
ated a veritable literary industry of critical texts. (Almost twenty
years ago, his biographer listed a bibliography of 600 texts written
about him. Since then the critical obsession with Nelligan has only
grown.)

Nelligan's life makes wonderful grist for both Freudian and historical mills. The son of an Irish immigrant father and a *pure laine*
Québécoise mother, he presents classic Oedipal and Two-Solitudes
complexes.

An inspector of postal services in the Gaspé, his intensely practical, unilingually-English father was often absent from the family home
in Montreal. ("Is that Irishman coming to visit us tomorrow?" Émile
once asked his mother when he was little.) The sensitive young boy
identified with his musically-gifted, patriotically *canadienne* mother,
going so far as to pronounce his name the French way and spelling it
"Nelighan."

When Nelligan was eighteen, his father tried to derail him from
his poetic aspirations, first by sending him on a sea voyage to Britain, then by finding him a job as a clerk. Neither ploy worked in the
desired manner. Nelligan threw himself all the more into his art,

but the inner turmoil which bore fruit in his oeuvre also unhinged him: the night of his greatest triumph as a poet, when he was borne through the streets of Montreal on the shoulders of his admirers, proved to be his last public appearance.

This drama unfolded on May 26, 1899 when, in response to some earlier criticism of his work by a visiting French critic, Nelligan gave a riveting recital of his newly-minted poem, "La Romance du vin." Nelligan's brief moment of glory at the end of one century and the dawn of another was symbolically timely: he was without question Canada's greatest nineteenth-century poet and, for reasons both of form and content, its first modern poet.

In three years, between the ages of sixteen and nineteen, Nelligan produced about 160 poems that were dramatically different from any written in this country before him. In nineteenth-century Quebec, patriotism, the glories of old France, ancestral fidelity to the land and Church were the accepted poetic themes. A poet was regarded as the mouthpiece of society's prevailing values.

In 1895, a group of students and intellectuals founded the École littéraire de Montréal, a literary society which met weekly to read poetry and discuss culture. Its honorary head was the establishment poet Louis Fréchette, but its most charismatic member would prove to be Nelligan, who joined in 1897.

Nelligan, in his exploration of unusual symbols, his sensitivity to the power of words, his musicality and his preoccupation with personal melancholy and alienation stood in dramatic contrast to Fréchette, the old-style poet laureate celebrating traditional values and historical themes. Nelligan looked for his inspiration to Edgar Allan Poe in the United States, and to French Romantic and symbolist poets such as Baudelaire, Rimbaud and Verlaine. He saw himself as a rebel artist with no other future than the writing of poetry. In "Un poète" he pleads, "Laissez-le vivre ainsi sans lui faire de mal!/ Laissez-le s'en aller; c'est un rêveur qui passe;/ C'est une âme angélique ouverte sur l'espace,/ Qui porte en elle un ciel de printemps auroral."

No one can say what it was that finally pushed him over the edge, what prompted him two months after his night of fame to climb a tree in St. Louis Square and threaten to kill himself. Shortly thereafter he was committed to the Retraite Saint-Benoît where he would remain for twenty-five years. In 1925, he was transferred to Saint-Jean-de-Dieu Hospital where he died in 1941.

Diagnosed as a schizophrenic, he produced no new work during his confinement. Yet he tried to write, keeping notebooks in which he jotted down poems by his favorite authors and attempted to revise his own work. A writer friend who visited him in 1909 observed that he continued to show "an undeviating obsession with literature."

Excerpt from "La Romance du vin," recited by Nelligan at his last public appearance, May 26, 1899. *Poésies complètes: 1896-1899,* edited by Luc Lacourcière (Montreal & Paris: Fides, 1952), 198-199.

> Tout se mêle en un vif éclat de gaîté verte,
> O le beau soir de mai! Tous les oiseaux en choeur,
> Ainsi que les espoirs naguères à mon coeur,
> Modulent leur prélude a ma croisée ouverte.
>
> O le beau soir de mai! le joyeux de mai!
> Un orgue au loin éclate en froides mélopées;
> Et les rayons, ainsi que de pourpres épées,
> Percent le couer du jour qui se meurt parfumé.
>
> Je suis gai! je suis gai! Dans le cristal qui chante,
> Verse, verse le vin! verse encore et toujours,
> Que je puisse oublier la tristesse des jours,
> Dans le dédain que j'ai de la foule méchante!
>
> Je suis gai! je suis gai! Vive le vin et l'Art!...
> J'ai le rêve de faire aussi des vers célèbres,
> Des vers qui gémiront les musiques funèbres
> Des vents d'automne au loin passant dans le brouillard.
> ....
> Les cloches ont chanté; le vent du soir odore...
> Et pendant que le vin ruisselle à joyeux flots,
> Je suis si gai, si gai, dans mon rire sonore,
> Oh! si gai, que j'ai peur d'éclater en sanglots!

STEPHEN LEACOCK

Portrait of the Professor as a Humorist

FEW THINGS are as hard to write as humour. Even Stephen Leacock (1869-1944), celebrated master of the absurd, the incongruous and the whimsical, and widely-known as a wit and practical joker from his college days, didn't try his hand at comic writing until he was over forty and had a best-selling book under his belt.

By then he had been a schoolmaster for ten years at Upper Canada College, his own boyhood school—and had hated it. The third of eleven children of a well-born but feckless father, he was born in England and came to Ontario with his family when he was six. He lived, in his own words, "a shadowed, tragic family life" on an Ontario farmstead dogged by debt and misery. His father abandoned them several times. Leacock's first biographer, Ralph L. Curry, tells the story of how Leacock, at seventeen, drove his father in a sleigh to the local railway station and, brandishing a whip, declared, "If you come back, I'll kill you."

Not, one would think, an auspicious start for a career in humour, in what would prove to be a rather unfunny time—from the lead-up to World War I, through the Depression and the era of World War II.

A career change in his thirties proved to be the making of Leacock. In 1899, he enrolled in graduate school at the University of Chicago, obtaining a doctorate in political economy and political science in 1903, when he was appointed a sessional lecturer at McGill.

The professorial life suited him, and in 1906 he published his first and most wildly-successful book which would be translated into nineteen languages: a college text entitled *Elements of Political Science*. Appointed head of the department of economics at McGill in 1908, his future was assured.

He became an unabashed lover of Montreal. ("The only paper from which a man can really get the news of the world in a shape that he can understand is the newspaper of his own 'home town,'" he wrote in 1922 in *My Discovery of England*. "For me, unless I can have the *Montreal Gazette* at my breakfast, and the *Montreal Star* at my dinner, I don't really know what is happening.")

Stephen Leacock would write some sixty books in the next four decades, about half of which were satire, parody or delicious nonsense, the other half essays, history, political science or polemics. (Often racist and sexist, he was a committed imperialist and conservative.)

His best work, according to Robertson Davies—another don, wit and prolific man of letters—" was the outpouring of genius." But, particularly at mid-career, he produced a long string of books that were mechanical and tedious, getting up at five in the morning to write when, observes Davies, "he would have done better to sit still and wait for an idea."

Oh, but when the muse did visit him, he was an unsurpassed master of parody and the one-liner (like the one about the knight who "flung himself upon his horse and rode madly off in all directions") and deft in his use of the literary sketch. Often compared to Dickens and Twain, like them he was a marvellous raconteur who spoke in a mildly self-deprecating and deceptively simple style and is best read out loud. The most famous Canadian author of his day, he lectured internationally and became a sort of unofficial ambassador for Montreal and McGill.

His two best works were *Sunshine Sketches of a Little Town*, a series of gently-satiric interrelated short stories loosely based on the Ontario town of Orillia where Leacock had a summer home, and *Arcadian Adventures with the Idle Rich*, a much harder-edged portrayal of hypocrisy, materialism and corruption in a large American city for which Montreal was in fact the model. These two books differ from the rest of his work in their unity of subject and theme. For the balance, he tended to produce an annual collection (timed to coincide with the Christmas trade) of anecdotes, parodies, monologues and humorous reflections that had appeared in magazines earlier in the year.

Alongside his phenomenal professional success (as well as making a literary fortune, he chalked up an impressive array of honorary degrees and prizes including a Governor General's Award in 1937), Leacock's personal life was scarred. His only son had an incurable illness; the wife to whom he was devoted left him a widower for almost twenty years; McGill, which had always commanded his loyalty and for which he had been such an unstinting unofficial publicist, insisted, to his great pain, on his compulsory retirement at sixty-five.

He died of throat cancer in 1944, in his seventy-fifth year.

Excerpt from Stephen Leacock's *Arcadian Adventures with the Idle Rich*, (Toronto: Gundy, 1914; McClelland & Stewart, New Canadian Library, 1959), 1-2.

The Mausoleum Club stands on the quietest corner of the best residential street in the City... About it are great elms trees with birds—the most expensive kind of birds—singing in the branches.

The street in the softer hours of the morning has an almost reverential quiet... The sunlight flickers through the elm trees, illuminating expensive nursemaids wheeling valuable children in little perambulators. Some of the children are worth millions and millions. In Europe, no doubt, you may see in the ... Champs Élysées a little prince or princess go past with a clattering military guard of honour. But that is nothing. It is not half so impressive, in the real sense, as what you may observe every morning on Plutoria Avenue beside the Mausoleum Club in the quietest part of the city. Here you may see a little toddling princess in a rabbit suit who owns fifty distilleries in her own right. There in a lacquered perambulator, sails past a little hooded head that controls from its cradle an entire New Jersey corporation... Incalculable infants wave their fifty-dollar rattles in an inarticulate greeting to one another...

...if you were to mount to the roof of the Mausoleum Club ... you could almost see the slums from there. But why should you? And on the other hand, if you never went up on the roof, but only dined inside among the palm trees, you would never know that the slums existed—which is much better...

SELECTED LEACOCK BIBLIOGRAPHY

Literary Lapses: A Book of Sketches (Montreal: Gazette, 1910).
Sunshine Sketches of a Little Town (Toronto: Bell & Cockburn, 1912; McClelland & Stewart, New Canadian Library, 1961).
Arcadian Adventures with the Idle Rich (Toronto: Gundy, 1914; McClelland & Stewart, New Canadian Library, 1959).
My Discovery of England (Toronto: Gundy, 1922; McClelland & Stewart, New Canadian Library, 1961).

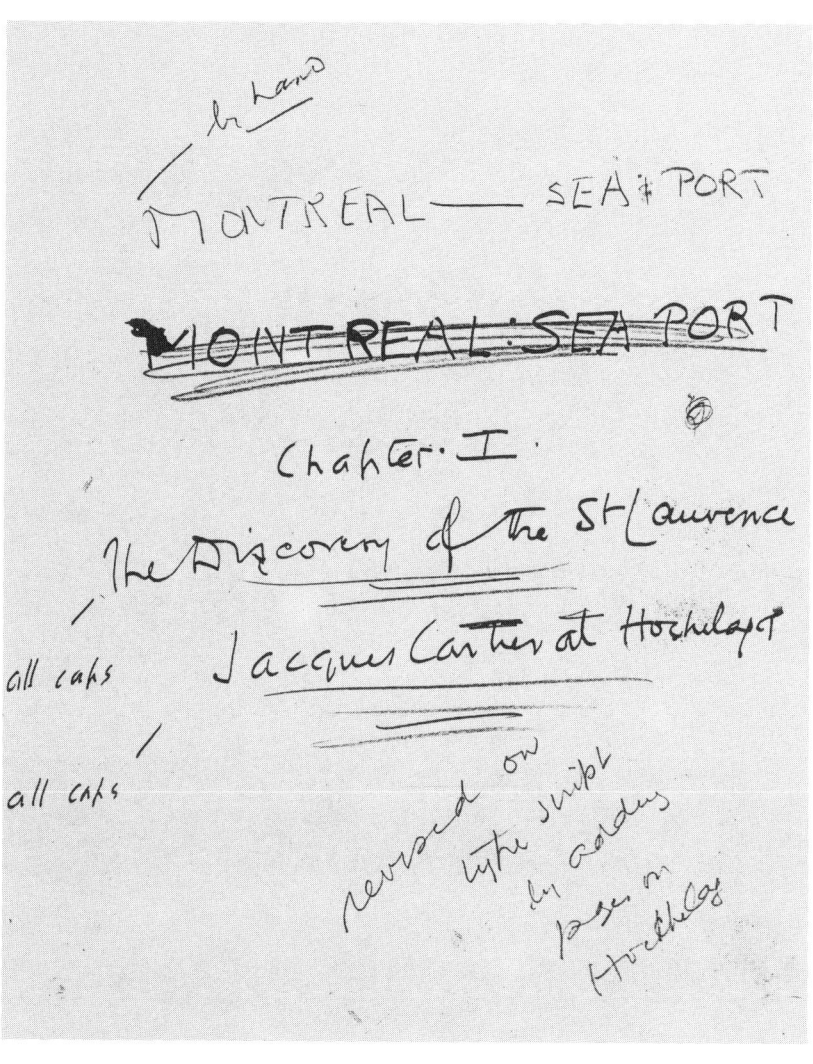

A manuscript page from Stephen Leacock's *Montreal: Seaport*
McGill University Archives

RINGUET

30 arpents

ROMAN

FLAMMARION

RINGUET

The Physician as Man of Letters

"I AM FIRST A DOCTOR AND THEN A WRITER," wrote Philippe Panetton (1895-1960) in 1939. "Literature interests me like a sport. It is a distraction in my leisure time."

He was a distinguished physician. In addition to a private practice as an ear, nose and throat specialist, he was on staff at Notre Dame Hospital in Montreal, a consultant at Saint-Eusèbe Hospital in Joliette, and taught in the faculty of medicine at Université de Montréal. In his spare time, under the pseudonym of "Ringuet"— his mother's family name—Panneton carried on a parallel literary career which might well excite the envy of most professional writers.

He produced journalism, verse, drama and parodies (one of his targets was the Abbé Lionel Groulx, whose *L'Appel de la race* he lampooned at a time when Groulx was a force to be reckoned with). His greatest achievement, the novel *Trente arpents*, won him the Prix de la Province de Québec, a Governor General's Award and a prize from the Académie Française. He produced two other novels, several works of non-fiction and a posthumously-published memoir entitled *Confidences*. A private journal of nearly 2,400 pages remains as yet unpublished.

Ringuet was born in Trois Rivières where his father, Ephrem Panneton, a descendant of a *vieille souche* habitant family, was a physician, and his mother, Eva Ringuet, an accomplished pianist. A poor student repeatedly thrown out of the classical college system, he was nonetheless a voracious reader who consistently excelled in French composition.

After a false professional start as a journalist, Ringuet entered medical school, studying in Quebec, Montreal and later in Paris. He returned to Montreal in 1923, and in the next fifteen years travelled, read and published widely. When *Trente arpents* (published by Flammarion in Paris) appeared in 1938, it was immediately acclaimed on both sides of the Atlantic as the first great French-Canadian novel and lauded as a masterpiece of literary realism.

Set firmly in the genre of the Québécois *roman de la terre* (Maria Chapdelaine springs immediately to mind), *Trente arpents* recounted the story of the Moisan family over four decades, from its rural roots in the Laurentians to chosen exile in the milltowns of New England. But it was a literary tour de force precisely because it transcended the tradition in which it was grounded. Whereas previous rural novels romanticized the countryside and vilified the city, *Trente arpents* drew a tragic portrait of a farmer beset by the forces of urbanization and technology and in conflict with a harsh and unforgiving land.

In its use of language, *Trente arpents* also broke new ground. Ringuet's blend of *joual* for dialogue and classical French for the narrative was something entirely new at the time.

His subsequent two novels were not on par with *Trente arpents*, but his non-fiction works were provocative and ahead of their time. In two books dealing with the discovery of America and with pre-Columbian civilizations, he condemned the treatment of native peoples by the conquerors and debunked the reputation of Columbus, attributing the "discovery" of America to Amerigo Vespucci.

An ardent defender of the French language, Ringuet took a pessimistic view of Quebec within Confederation. He saw political separation as unlikely but, in its absence, regarded the disappearance of the French language as practically inevitable. These opinions did not stand in the way of his acceptance of a Canadian diplomatic posting: in 1956 he became ambassador to Portugal and died there in 1960.

A popular and engaging man, Ringuet was, in the opinion of his biographer Jean Panneton, an essentially enigmatic figure who, though granting countless interviews, always held something of himself back. His voluminous unpublished diary may yet yield up secrets.

Excerpt from Ringuet's *Trente arpents* (1938), translated as *Thirty Acres* by Felix and Dorothea Walter (Toronto: Macmillan, 1940), 320-321.

Exiled to New England, the aging patriarch Euchariste Moisan is forced to work as a janitor in a garage, having abandoned his thirty acres of land in the Laurentians:

So every night he set off for the garage and shut himself up until morning among all those mechanical monsters crouching like wild animals in a cage.

Gradually, without his knowing how or why, he began to lose hope. It seemed to him that his Laurentian homeland was getting further and further away every day and was becoming a province in the realm of the unattainable. He felt that each one of the hours he had lived through since he left was an infinity, an eternity he could never hope to retrace.

The fine weather was over. The autumn rains had come again, those cold and endless October downpours that mark the end of another cycle and the temporary divorce of sun and earth during which the farmer is useless.

In June, enjoying the first hot weather, he kept saying: "Dandy weather for the hay."

When in July it didn't rain for two weeks, he reflected: "If it don't rain in a few days the oats won't be so good."...

But now that autumn had returned, there was nothing in his past life that found an echo in his thoughts....

EARTH
AND
HIGH HEAVEN

A NOVEL BY
GWETHALYN GRAHAM

GWETHALYN GRAHAM
Novelist and Social Crusader

SHE WON her first Governor General's Award for fiction when she was only twenty-five and followed it up with another for her second novel six years later. *Earth and High Heaven*, the second book, was set in Montreal and became an international bestseller. Translated into nine languages, it sold 1,250,000 copies and made of its author an overnight sensation. Yet few people today remember Gwethalyn Graham, who lived and worked in Montreal for many years, and died here in 1965.

The runaway critical and popular success of *Earth and High Heaven* is particularly surprising when its subject is taken into account. Published in 1944 during a period of pervasive Canadian anti-Semitism (asked in 1945 how many Jews would be allowed into Canada when the war ended, a senior Canadian official responded, "None is too many") and as the horrors of the Holocaust were gradually unfolding, it recounted a star-crossed love story between a Westmount socialite and a small-town Ontario Jew. The book was, except for its happy ending, largely based on Graham's personal experience.

Gwethalyn Graham was born in Toronto in 1913 into a socially-prominent and liberal family. Her mother was a leader in the Canadian women's suffrage movement; her maternal grandfather, whom she adored, "would not tolerate the use of any of the derogatory slang words which label national or religious groups"; her father was a cultured lawyer. Graham had a privileged upbringing which included attendance at Toronto's posh all-girls Havergal College, a finishing school in Lausanne and a year at prestigious Smith College in Massachusetts.

But she had first hand acquaintanceship with pain as well. Of ungainly stature and size, she suffered a great deal in school. She eloped in her second year at college at age nineteen, only to be abandoned by her husband before their baby was a year old.

She moved to Montreal, a city she loved, in 1934 with her son (she was twenty-one), and began to write. From the first her fiction concerned itself with issues of justice, tolerance and international understanding. *Swiss Sonata*, her first novel, was loosely based on her Swiss-boarding school experiences and portrayed a cosmopolitan cast of girls against the politically menacing background of the 1930s. The book went through two British editions, received favourable reviews in the United States, Britain and Canada, won the Governor General's Award and was banned in Germany.

Following Swiss Sonata's publication, Graham travelled in Europe for six months in 1938 and returned to Canada passionately committed to assisting Jews seeking refuge from the gathering storm. She wrote two well-researched articles on the subject for *Saturday Night* magazine, circulated petitions and made speeches. While on this social crusade in Toronto, she fell in love with a Canadian Jewish lawyer. When her father refused to meet him, the romance ended.

Earth and High Heaven, which Graham subsequently wrote in Montreal, is a heartfelt novel in which romantic love challenges bigotry in war-time Canada. Erica Drake of the "Westmount Drakes," an affluent and enlightened family, is devastated to discover that her cultivated father will not hear of her love for Marc Reiser who is, but for his Jewish background, eminently suitable for her. A compelling attack on covert anti-Semitism, the novel's strongest elements are the father-daughter conflict and the dark machinations resorted to by Charles Drake in his opposition to the match.

Graham found the success of *Earth and High Heaven* so paralyzing she never wrote fiction again (she collaborated with Solange Chaput-Rolland on *Dear Enemy*, a 1963 work of non-fiction dedicated to understanding between French and English-Canadians). A second marriage in 1947 took her away from Montreal to the United States, only to return here in 1958 after it also failed. She died of cancer at age fifty-two.

Graham has not fared well with many latter-day critics whose indictment of *Earth and High Heaven* as shallow and patronizing probably accounts for her relative obscurity today. Nearly fifty years after its first publication, it is unquestionably somewhat dated, but its shining sincerity and strong characterizations still make it an absorbing read. One can understand why, with the injection of the tragic timeliness of its day, it captured the public imagination.

Excerpt from *Earth and High Heaven* by Gwethalyn Graham (London: Cape, 1944; Toronto: McClelland & Stewart, New Canadian Library, 1969), 147-149.

Charles Drake could not imagine what Marc Reiser's family would be like. The fact that their son was presentable enough on the surface proved nothing, since there was an extraordinary difference between the first and the second generation. He remembered what a shock he had had when the parents of a Jewish importer whom he had known for years and had always regarded as quite exceptional, the very best type of Jew ... what a shock he had had when the fellow's parents had turned out to be pure ghetto. The old man wore a black skull cap, both he and his wife kept dropping into Yiddish....

Charles Drake was almost beside himself.

At breakfast, at dinner and in the evenings when Erica was at home, he would suddenly start in on the Jews again and go on talking, talking, talking; he said anything that came into his head without fully realizing what he was saying, except that he was careful never to refer to Marc directly. It was as though everything he had ever heard against the Jews, back to his earliest childhood, was coming out all in a period of a few weeks, five, ten or fifteen minutes at a time, during which he would keep his eyes fixed on Erica, searching her face to see if at least he had succeeded in making an impression.

He did not succeed; he failed altogether.... She knew Marc, she was in possession of the evidence, of the actual facts concerning Marc Reiser, and between those facts and her father's statements about Jews, there was simply no connection.

A. M. K L E I N

Poetic Genius

IN HIS INTRODUCTION to Abraham Moses Klein's first collection of poems, *Hath Not a Jew...*, the critic Ludwig Lewisohn described the book's young author as "the first contributor of authentic Jewish poetry to the English language." Glowing as this praise was, it fell short of truth. For A.M. Klein (1909-72) was arguably the most important English-Canadian writer in the first half of this century, a genius with words whose profound knowledge of Judaica was twinned to a genuinely Canadian sensibility. Abe Klein wrote out of the wellspring of his Jewishness with a virtuosity fostered by the unique linguistic environment of Montreal where his ear had grown attuned to the resonances of Yiddish and Hebrew, English and French.

Born in Ratno in Ukraine, Klein came to Montreal as a baby in 1910 with his family. He grew up in the heyday of Yiddish culture in the ghetto of Montreal—a world now largely lost—rooted in Jewish tradition from which, though he eventually modified his orthodoxy, he never broke away. ("Not sole was I born, but entire genesis:/For to the fathers that begat me, this/Body is residence," he wrote in "A Psalm Touching Genealogy.")

Klein attended Baron Byng, Montreal's Protestant-School-Board-run, quintessentially Jewish high school, where his best friend was David Lewis, future leader of the New Democratic Party. He tutored Irving Layton, another good friend, in Latin, in nearby Fletcher's Field. Layton has said, "hearing Klein roll off the Virgilian hexameters in a beautiful orotund voice that rose above the traffic

... I realized how very lovely the sound of poetry could be."

Klein went on to McGill University where he was associated with the McGill Movement of poets, the best known among whom were F.R. Scott and A.J.M. Smith. The 1920s were his most prolific period and his first poems were published in the *McGill Daily*. Upon graduation, he chose law school at the Université de Montréal over McGill. His poetry would later show a deep sympathy and understanding of French-Canadian society, and in diction and cadence poems like "Montreal" bear the obvious stamp of the French language: "Splendour erablic of your promenades/Foliates there, and there your maisonry/Of pendant balcon and escalier'd march,/ Unique midst English habitat,/Is vivid Normandy!"

Klein graduated from law school to the financial woes of the Depression, compounded in his case by an early marriage (in 1935, to his high school sweetheart, Bessie Kozlov) and the subsequent birth of three children. In the late 1930s, his law practice languishing, he took over the editorship of the *Canadian Jewish Chronicle*, then the leading English-Jewish weekly in Canada. In the seventeen years that he was the *Chronicle*'s editor, he played a significant role in shaping opinion in the Canadian-Jewish community by vigorously denouncing anti-Semitism during the dark war years and by promoting Zionism afterwards.

Financial pressures must have induced him in the same period to take on the thankless, if lucrative, job of speechwriter and publicist for Samuel Bronfman, a position which had him churning out company reports and doggerel for Bronfman family occasions (Klein is widely regarded to be the model for the L.B. Berger character in Mordecai Richler's *Solomon Gursky Was Here*).

This brilliant and many faceted man also ran (unsuccessfully) for Parliament as a CCF candidate, lectured in the English Department at McGill, wrote short stories, essays and criticism (his uncompleted commentary on Joyce's *Ulysses* has received much praise) and was a veritable genius at translation from Hebrew and Yiddish into English.

But his greatest achievements were as a poet and visionary novelist: his masterpiece, the innovative novel, *The Second Scroll*. For his 1944 collection, *The Rocking Chair and Other Poems*, he won a Governor General's Award; for the totality of his oeuvre, the Lorne Pierce medal of the Royal Society of Canada.

Any summation of Klein's work is of necessity reductive, but in *The Rocking Chair* collection he found his true voice in trilingual puns, culturally diverse imagery and metaphor, subtle rhythms and a perspective that was both highly personal and extraordinarily varied.

Published in 1951, *The Second Scroll* resulted in part from a trip Klein made on assignment for the *Canadian Jewish Chronicle* in 1949 to displaced persons camps in Europe and to the newly-created state of Israel. The slim, richly allusive novel that the trip inspired took as its subject nothing less than the history and destiny of the Jewish people, in a form that parallelled the "first scroll": the Torah and its commentaries. A blazing triumph of language, it was a celebration of Zionism and the capacity for human renewal in the face of total depravity and destruction.

The writer of this impassioned and triumphant poetic narrative battled despair and self-disgust for large chunks of his life. Though critics and fellow poets lionized him, his work was not easily accessible and he felt the neglect of the general public as a personal failure.

In 1954 he suffered a nervous breakdown from which he never fully recovered. He gave up his law practice and editorship and became increasingly reclusive.

For the last eighteen years of his life he did not write a word.

Excerpt from "Autobiographical" in Gloss Aleph of *The Second Scroll* by A.M. Klein (New York: Knopf, 1951; Toronto: McClelland & Stewart, New Canadian Library, 1968), 95-97.

    Out of the ghetto streets where a Jewboy
    Dreamed pavement into pleasant Bible-land,
    Out of the Yiddish slums where childhood met
    The friendly beard, the loutish Sabbath-goy,
    Or followed, proud, the Torah-escorting band,
    Out of the jargoning city I regret,

Rise memories, like sparrows rising from
The gutter-scattered oats,
Like sadness sweet of synagogal hum,
Like Hebrew violins
Sobbing delight upon their Eastern notes.

Again they ring their little bells, those doors
Deemed by the tender-year'd, magnificent:
Old Ashkenazi's cellar, sharp with spice;
The widows' double-parlored candy-stores
And nuggets sweet bought for one sweaty cent;
The warm fresh-smelling bakery, its pies,
Its cakes, its navel'd bellies of black bread;
The lintels candy-poled
Of barber-shop, bright-bottled, green, blue, red;
And fruit-stall piled, exotic,
And the big synagogue door, with letters of gold.

Again my kindergarten home is full—
Saturday night—with kin and compatriot:
My brothers playing Russian card-games; my
Mirroring sisters looking beautiful,
Humming the evening's imminent fox-trot;
My uncle Mayer, of blessed memory,
Still murmuring maariv, counting holy words;
And the two strangers, come
Fiery from Volhynia's murderous hordes—
The cards and humming stop.
And I too swear revenge for that pogrom.

...

I am no old man fatuously intent
On memoirs, but in memory I seek
The strength and vividness of nonage days,
Not tranquil recollection of event.
It is a fabled city that I seek;

It stands in Space's vapours and Time's haze;
Thence comes my sadness in remembered joy
Constrictive of the throat;
Thence do I hear, as heard by a Jewboy,
The Hebrew violins,
Delighting in the sobbed Oriental note.

F. R. SCOTT

Renaissance Man
of the Twentieth Century

IN AN ARTICLE EULOGIZING F.R. SCOTT, Hugh MacLennan wrote in 1985 that it was hard to believe the perennially youthful Scott had been born in the last year of the nineteenth century, though—MacLennan added—Scott considered himself to be the last of the nineteenth-century idealists.

Frank Scott was so many-sided—a poet, constitutional lawyer, professor, civil libertarian, social democrat, political theorist and activist—and had such a profound influence on Canadian artistic and political culture that he has been called the most remarkable Canadian of his generation. Idealism was the common denominator of his drive and accomplishments.

Francis Reginald Scott (1899-1985) was born in Quebec City, the sixth of seven children of an Anglican Archdeacon who himself wrote poetry and from whom the son inherited both a deep love of nature and a belief in public service. Educated in Quebec City, Bishop's University in Lennoxville and Oxford (as a Rhodes scholar), Scott turned away from his early religious feelings, transmuting them into socialism. He returned from England to Canada in 1923 to teach at Lower Canada College and to write poetry, but he soon entered McGill Law School.

At McGill he met the poet and critic A.J.M. Smith who became a lifelong friend and with whom he founded the McGill Movement which gave birth to an influential literary magazine, the *McGill Fortnightly Review*. Leon Edel, future biographer of Henry James, and the poets John Glassco, A.M. Klein and Leo Kennedy were also associated with the group.

Throughout the 1920s and 1930s Scott increasingly began to turn to Canadian sources of inspiration for both his poetic and political values. As with the Group of Seven in painting, the Canadian landscape became a source of national pride and identity and a subject of art for him. ("Laurentian Shield" begins, for instance, with the majestic vision, "Hidden in wonder and snow, or sudden with summer,/This land stares at the sun in a huge silence".)

At about the same time, he was developing an iconoclastic wit that satirized the pettifogging imitativeness of the Canadian literary world as in "The Canadian Authors Meet": "Expansive puppets percolate self-unction/Beneath a portrait of the Prince of Wales./...O Canada, O Canada, O can/A day go by without new authors springing/To paint the native maple, and to plan/More ways to set the selfsame welkin ringing?"

In 1928 Scott married the distinguished painter Marian Dale (their son, Peter Dale Scott is also a gifted poet) and joined the staff of McGill Law School where he eventually served as dean from 1961-64.

As a constitutional jurist he would win three landmark decisions at the Supreme Court in two of which he tangled with Quebec premier Maurice Duplessis. Scott led the legal attack against the Padlock Act, which Duplessis had introduced in 1937 permitting the police to padlock the premises of anyone thought to be a Communist. He then took on the case of Roncarelli vs Duplessis, in defence of Jehovah's Witnesses, as a matter of principle though he had no ideological fondness for the sect. In the third case, Scott quipped "I went to bat for the Lady Chatte" and succeeded in lifting the ban in Quebec of D. H. Lawrence's *Lady Chatterley's Lover* on charges of obscenity.

Running parallel with his writing, teaching and legal careers, Scott was in on the ground floor in the founding of the socialist movement in Canada with J.S. Woodsworth, Frank Underhill and David

Lewis. He was president of the Montreal branch of the League for Social Reconstruction in 1932, one of the framers of the Regina Manifesto and national chairman for eight years of the Co-operative Commonwealth Federation that became the precursor of the New Democratic Party.

For more than forty years Scott's Westmount home on Clarke Avenue was a meeting place for Montreal literati of both languages. A gifted translator of French poetry, he stimulated contact between English and French writers.

He believed that, indeed, poetry can help to change society, and much of his work has a political thrust. In "Natural Resources" he wrote, "Come and see the vast natural wealth of this mine./In the short space of ten years/It has produced six American millionaires/ And two thousand pauperized Canadian families." More subtle but no less devastating, in "W.L.M.K." he deliciously sent up William Lyon Mackenzie King: "He skilfully avoided what was wrong/Without saying what was right,/And never let his on the one hand/Know what his on the other was doing."

Among his many honours, in his "retirement" Scott won three Governor General's Awards for three retrospective volumes: the translation prize for his *Poems of French Canada*; the non-fiction prize for *Essays on the Constitution*; and the prize for poetry for his *Collected Poems*.

Nothwithstanding the breadth of Scott's achievements, Hugh MacLennan wrote of him, "Frank often said that he would like to be remembered best as a poet."

From Scott's *Collected Poems* (Toronto: McClelland & Stewart, 1981), two samples: one serious, the other playful.

PRISON (p. 143)

In Fullum Street gaol
In the nineteen hundred and fiftieth year of the Christian era
Insane women, locked in filthy cells,
Scream and howl unattended.
(See the Montreal Herald for February the second.)

At the Ritz the Bach Partita
Is the more exquisite because it can come
Out of such a world.
I too scream in my cell,
For my own inattention
Built their gaol, my prison,
In the far reaches of the inner mind.

BONNE ENTENTE (p. 256)

("One man's meat is another man's poisson."— A. Lismer)

The advantages of living with two cultures
Strike one at every turn,
Especially when one finds a notice in an office building
"This elevator will not run on Ascension Day";
Or reads in the *Montreal Star*:
"Tomorrow being the Feast of the Immaculate Conception,
There will be no collection of garbage in the city";
Or sees on the restaurant menu the bilingual dish:
DEEP APPLE PIE
TARTE AUX POMMES PROFONDES

Irving Layton, F.R. Scott and Louis Dudek, 5 March 1983
at book launching for *CIV/n: A Literary Magazine of the 50s.*

AGAGUK

~~TOUNDRA~~

CHAPITRE UN

Quand il eut atteint l'âge et prouvé sa vaillance, ~~il~~ *Agaguk* prit une
outre d'eau et un quartier de viande séchée, puis il partit à travers le pays
qui était celui de la toundra sans fin, plate et unie comme un ciel d'hiver,
sans horizon et sans arbres.

Il trouva les endroits ~~xxxxxxx~~ *propices* d'un pied habité, ~~Il~~ évita les
terriers de ratons, et, quand il eut trouvé un monticule sans faille et de fond
solide, il le parcourut en deux sens pour le bien mesurer, *puis il* planta les deux bâtons
et dressa l'abri de grosse toile qu'il avait apportés sur son dos.

Plus tard, aux neiges venues, il construirait un igloo.

Il passa une semaine dans les parages. Il ~~étudia~~ *fallait étudier* toutes les pistes,
~~Il~~ scruter le ciel, ~~Il~~ observer les vents et la marche des nuages.

Il creusa la toundra avec son couteau, un trou grand comme une soupiè-
re et l'eau vint couvrir le fond. *Ce serait suffisant pour survivre* ~~Ce n'était pas un puits, mais aux temps d'été,~~
~~l'on a encore les réserves de neige fondue, mises en outre. C'est seulement vers~~
~~la fin, quand il fait chaud même sur la toundra, que l'eau peut manquer.~~

~~Ici, il en viendrait assez pour survivre.~~

Durant la semaine, ~~Agaguk~~ *Agaguk* prit six renards dans les collets qu'il
tendit, deux ratons, et quand un cariboo ~~passa trop~~ *vint* près du monticule, ~~Agaguk~~ *il*
l'abattit d'une seule balle.

Il fuma une partie de la viande, pour le voyage de retour; ~~et puis~~ *ensuite*
il éparpilla les restes à la ronde, pour habituer les renards et les loups à
venir manger près du monticule.

Puis il retourna au village, ~~xxxxxxxxxxx~~ cent milles plus haut
vers les neiges, afin de mettre ~~xx xxxxxxxxxxxxxxxxxxxx~~ à exécution le projet
qu'il avait.

YVES THÉRIAULT

Prolific Primitivist

FRENCH CANADA'S MOST PROLIFIC AND VERSATILE WRITER of serious fiction started out as a high school dropout. The boy who quit school at fifteen in grade eight to work as a cheese vendor, bartender and truck driver, who fought off tuberculosis and—much later—the effects of a debilitating stroke, would in the course of his life produce an astounding literary output: some forty novels, more than 1,000 short stories, science fiction and detective collections, tales for children, works of erotica, articles, essays, plays and 1,300 radio and television scripts. Self-taught and unconventional, Yves Thériault (1915-83) is virtually unmatched in Canadian literature for his eclectic interests and restless spirit of experimentation.

Thériault is best known for his novel *Agaguk* (1958, recently made into a film), the stark and authentic tale of a young Inuit couple in the *pays d'en haut* for which he won international recognition and both the Prix de la Province de Québec and the Prix France-Canada. *Agaguk* was the first of a series of books with an anthropological orientation in which Thériault championed native people and decried their assimilation. In 1960 he also won a Governor General's Award for *Ashini*, a lyrical novel celebrating the Montagnais.

One quarter Montagnais himself, he spoke Cree yet cannot be narrowly identified with any single ethnic group. A relentless critic of French-Canadian xenophobia, he was an ardent defender of immigrants and minority cultures.

Thériault was born in Quebec City in 1915 of mixed Acadian,

Montagnais and Québécois ancestry. When he was three, his car-penter father moved the family to Montreal where the construction business was booming at the time. He grew up in Notre Dame de Grâce, learning a perfect English and settling later in his adult life on Girouard Street. Curious and rebellious from childhood on, he sometimes attended synagogue with Jewish friends from whom he picked up Yiddish and Hebrew. (One of his earliest and best novels, *Aaron*, explores the assimilation into the Montreal anglophone com-munity of a young orthodox Jew.) His extraordinary openness to diverse cultural influences was also fostered by wide-ranging travel.

Thériault served an unusual apprenticeship as a writer. Often grotesque and shocking, his writing implies first hand knowledge of seaminess and violence. His odd jobs as tractor salesman, trapper and nightclub emcee eventually gave way to radio and television work and public relations. By the mid-1960s he had become a re-spected spokesman for native people and director of the cultural portfolio of the Ministry of Indian Affairs in Ottawa.

He started writing radio scripts and short stories in the 1940s. In 1945 he answered an ad in *La Presse* calling for writers of "10 cent stories" of thirty-two pages each. He and his wife, Germaine-Michelle Blanchet, each undertook to manufacture anonymously or pseudonymously three detective stories and three romances a week. (At one point, Thériault's output grew to eleven stories a week.) With such training in speedwriting, it is perhaps not startling that in 1968 he was able to complete six books, four of them novels. Nor is it surprising that he has been criticized for careless and hasty prose.

Struggle—be it against a hostile northern landscape, a rigid pa-rental figure, or a repressive power—is the common denominator linking Thériault's diverse subjects. He wrote with an almost brutal simplicity about sex, nature, death and the search for individuality. With much of his work as yet still unpublished, critics are unwilling to pronounce on the overall quality of his work.

Yet, had he written nothing but *Agaguk*, it alone would have as-sured his reputation. The novel tells the story of a young Inuit hunter, *Agaguk*, and his wife, Iriook, as they battle to survive on their own away from their tribal village. Set in the 1930s, it dramatizes the conflict between ancient and cruel tribalism and modern ways without drawing simplistic conclusions. In it, the tundra wilderness assumes a haunting presence and the young protagonists an almost epic grandeur. The book is widely studied in both community colleges and universities, and Thériault has been hailed as one of the giants of Quebec literature.

Indeed, there was nothing small about him.

Excerpt from *Agaguk* by Yves Thériault, first published in 1958, translated by Miriam Chapin (Toronto: McGraw-Hill Ryerson, 1967), 224-225. In the last chapter of the novel, Agaguk's wife, Iriook, gives birth to their second child.

His hands extended, Agaguk waited to grasp the child, then suddenly in a final effort the new being slid and fell into them. With a sure motion he cut the cord with an ivory knife. Higher up, very far it seemed from Agaguk, Iriook was moaning—so far that the man heard nothing of it. A great buzzing was in his ears; he stayed squatting, holding the child. He had eyes only for its sex.

A girl!

It was now or never. He must take advantage of Iriook's semi-consciousness, of the baby's momentary quiet.

Agaguk crawled like an animal, holding the slimy body with one hand. Silently he made his way toward the tunnel. He knew what to do. Once outside, he would strangle the girl with a decisive motion, breaking its neck at the same time. Then he would throw the body in the snow. The wolves and the dogs would quickly feed on it, and in the morning nothing would be left...

Agaguk was just reaching the tunnel when suddenly Iriook's voice, calm and implacable, was raised.

"Agaguk!"

He froze. The child against him still did not move. He turned his head. The woman was sitting up. Rifle in hand she was aiming at him.

"Now make her breathe," she said.

Aaron (Quebec: Institut Littéraire du Quebec, 1958).

Agaguk (Quebec: Institut Littéraire du Quebec, 1958), translated by Miriam Chapin (Toronto: Ryerson, 1963).

Ashini (Montreal: Fides, 1960), translated by Gwendolyn Moore (Montreal: Harvest House, 1972).

La femme Anna et autres contest (Montreal: VLB, 1981).

HUBERT AQUIN

Gentle Terrorist, Tormented Genius

ON MARCH 15, 1977 at the age of forty-seven, Hubert Aquin—variously described as "the greatest novelist of modern Quebec," "a literary saint," "a national hero," and "the most intelligent writer in the Francophone world"—took a shotgun that had belonged to his late father and, in the peaceful grounds of Villa Maria, a private Catholic girls' school in Notre Dame de Grâce, raised it to his mouth and killed himself.

It was perhaps the only imaginable ending for the darkly brilliant artist of paradox and contradiction whose last and greatest novel, *Neige noire* (translated into English as *Hamlet's Twin*), begins with a quotation from Kierkegaard, "I must now both be and not be."

Aquin's extraordinary first published novel, *Prochain épisode* (an earlier, previously rejected work, *L'Invention de la mort*, was recently discovered and published), burst upon the literary scene in 1965 with the force of the bombs that were in those days erupting from Montreal mailboxes. Aquin (1929-77) had joined the Rassemblement pour l'indépendance nationale (RIN) five years earlier (he held executive positions in the party from 1963-68). In 1964, after announcing to the press that he was about to join an underground terrorist movement, he was arrested in possession of a gun and in a stolen car. Upon pleading temporary insanity, he was trans-

ferred from jail to the Albert Prévost Psychiatric Institute for obser-
vation. During the four months' wait for his case to come to trial
(he was eventually acquitted), he wrote *Prochain épisode*, the story
of a young separatist awaiting trial and writing an espionage story in
the psychiatric ward of the Montreal prison where he has been de-
tained.

The book was instantly hailed a masterpiece. ("God be thanked,"
declared establishment critic Jean-Éthier Blais, "Our great writer at
last.") The author of this disturbing, angry and obsessed novel was
a slender, quiet young man with sensitive features and a demeanour
difficult to reconcile with terrorism.

He grew up in the Parc Lafontaine area of Montreal, the son of a
sporting goods clerk and his wife. Aquin's education included attendance at l'École Olier (Émile Nelligan's elementary school),
l'Université de Montréal, where he studied philosophy, and l'Institut
d'Études politiques in Paris.

When he returned from Paris at the age of twenty-six, he pursued
a varied career as a journalist, a producer at Radio-Canada and a
scriptwriter and film director for the National Film Board, experiences that he would incorporate into the three novels he wrote after
Prochain épisode.

All of them bear strong cinematographic influences.

Neige noire (1974), in particular, is his final struggle to make of
the novel a total art-form. Its complex structure encompasses a
movie scenario within which is staged a television production of the
play *Hamlet*. In it, as well as in *Trou de mémoire* (1968; translated as
Blackout) and in *L'Antiphonaire* (1969; translated as *The Antiphonary*),
Aquin stretches the confines of the novel form and involves the reader
in a process of co-creation that is both exhilarating and exacting.
His aim is nothing less than the incorporation into literature of the
full force of visual, sound and mythic evocation that would seem to
be the preserve of cinema.

Although *Neige noire* is regarded as Aquin's finest book, *Prochain
épisode* is the most accessible and the only one not marred by the
violent sex and often gratuitous sado-pornography for which critics
have often taken him to task. He acknowledged the literary influence of James Joyce, Vladimir Nabokov and the detective novel genre

in general to which he was addicted.

Aquin's life was fuelled by a series of uncompromising gestures of independence. In 1968 he broke with the RIN when it merged with René Lévesque's Mouvement Souveraineté-Association to form the Parti Québécois. (He described the merger as "suicidal" for the independence movement.) In 1971 he resigned from the editorial board of the magazine *Liberté* which he had founded, accusing his colleagues of selling out to the Canada Council and the federal government. In 1976, he quit his position of literary director of Éditions La Presse after accusing Roger Lemelin, editor of *La Presse*, in an open letter to *Le Devoir*, of "colonizing Quebec from within."

He became the first francophone Quebec writer to refuse a Governor General's Award (in 1969, for *Trou de mémoire*. Leonard Cohen also refused the award that year for *Selected Poems 1956-1968*.)

A tormented genius who saw his life as a conscious metaphor for Quebec history, Aquin dictated a note to his wife, Andrée Yanacopoulo, on the day of his death. She interpreted the source of his tragedy to be writer's block.

He declared his death a free and positive choice.

"I have lived intensely and now it is over."

Excerpt from Hubert Aquin's *Prochain Épisode*, translated by Penny Williams (McClelland & Stewart, New Canadian Library, 1972), 69-71.

The meaning of this novel will not be the shattering novelty of its final format. I am this book from hour to hour and day to day; as long as I don't commit suicide I have no intention of stopping. This disorderly book and I, we are the same.... An episode is born every time I sit down to write. Every writing session is a singular event in itself, and only forms a novel to the extent that I bind myself to my shattered past. An event of its own, my book writes me. It can only be understood within the historical drama in which it belongs. Suddenly I dream of my disordered epic becoming part of the national calendar of a people without history! What derision, what pity! It is true we have no history. Our history will begin at the unknown moment when the revolutionary war begins. Our history will inaugurate itself in the blood of the revolution which crushes me and which I have poorly served. That day, with open veins, we will enter the world.... History will begin when we bring to our illness the rhythm and fire of war. Everything will take on the flamboyant colour of history when we march to combat, sub-machine guns in hand. When our brothers die in the ambushes and our sisters are alone to salute June 24, then our writing will cease to be an event and become an account....

SELECTED BIBLIOGRAPHY

Prochain épisode (Montreal: Cercle du Livre de France, 1965), translated by Penny Williams (Toronto: McClelland & Stewart, 1967).
Trou de mémoire (Montreal: Cercle du Livre de France, 1968), translated by Alan Brown as *Blackout* (Toronto: Anansi, 1974).
L'Antiphonaire (Montreal, Cercle du Livre de France, 1969), translated by Alan Brown as *The Antiphonary* (Toronto: Anansi, 1973).
Neige noire (Montreal: La Presse, 1974), translated by Sheila Fischman as *Hamlet's Twin* (Toronto, McClelland & Stewart, 1979).

GABRIELLE ROY

Enchantment and Sorrow

A PENNILESS FREELANCE JOURNALIST selling articles here and there in 1941, Gabrielle Roy lived a marginal existence in a rooming house on Dorchester Street, near Greene Avenue. "For human warmth," she told Donald Cameron many years later, "I used to roam the streets, walk and walk and walk."

"I used to choose as the goal of my walks," she said elsewhere, "the pretty avenues of Westmount and the slope of the mountain. One day, by pure chance, by caprice if you will, I instead went south on rue Saint-Ambroise and found myself before I knew it in the very heart of Saint-Henri. What can I say? How can I give you the deep impression I suddenly received? It was like the lightning that strikes lovers; it was a revelation, an illumination."

Gabrielle Roy (1909-83) was so convinced that a novel set in the working-class world of Saint-Henri was crying out to be written that she feared someone else would get there before her. Though *Bonheur d'occasion* (later translated as *The Tin Flute*) would not be published until 1945, Roy began immediately to bring the district to life in a series of articles for one of her freelance markets, the *Bulletin des agriculteurs*, a farm publication.

Bonheur d'occasion would go on to sell over a million copies, win a Governor General's Award and become a Literary Guild of America selection. It made of Roy the first Canadian winner of the prestigious French Prix Fémina and a recipient of the Lorne Pierce Medal of the Royal Society of Canada. (She subsequently won many other awards including two more Governor General's prizes.) Critics have judged it a landmark in the development of the contemporary Québécois novel because of its innovative subject matter (the grittiness of urban life) and its freshness of language—Roy's use of *joual*, "le langage canayen."

Yet Gabrielle Roy, though passionate in her love of Montreal and Quebec, was a latecomer to the province and never felt comfortable with the label of Québécoise, French-Canadian or even Canadian writer. Once she had committed herself to a writing career, she set out to make a world class reputation for herself, just as, she wrote in her autobiography, she yearned for her home to be "the whole world and all mankind."

Roy was the youngest of eleven children (eight of whom survived to adulthood) born in St. Boniface, Manitoba to an impoverished couple who had moved there from Quebec. She was very close to her mother who nourished her from infancy on stories of the Quebec homeland. Roy experienced at an early age the petty and not-so-petty humiliations of being francophone on the prairies. Yet she became so completely bilingual that at one point she considered making English her language of composition. In the end, she wrote in French but all her books were translated almost immediately into English and she achieved wide recognition throughout the English-speaking world as well as in France and Quebec.

Her reputation suffered in Quebec towards the end of her life because of her refusal to become politically engaged on the side of indépendantisme. In a 1971 interview she said, "My great hope would be that Quebec would realize itself fully as a distinct part of Canada, and stay Canadian, bringing to Canada a part of its richness." Beyond that she maintained, "The main engagement of the writer is towards truthfulness; therefore he must keep his mind and his judgement free."

Roy's breadth of vision was born under the limitless prairie sky that she loved, then left at the age of twenty-eight, after having taught school for eight years in Manitoba. She travelled to England (where she at first thought to make an actress of herself) and France in the late 1930s, tasting the magic of Europe and the pain of a broken love affair.

She found her vocation as a novelist when she returned to Canada in 1939 and began writing *Bonheur d'occasion* in Montreal. After its publication, she married a physician from St. Boniface, Dr. Marcel Carbotte, and went abroad for another three years. She subsequently settled in Quebec City and wrote some sixteen books: novels, short stories, children's books, a collection of essays, and an exquisite autobiography, *Enchantment and Sorrow*.

Bonheur d'occasion, a work notable for its naturalism and its tone of somber social desperation, was followed in 1950 by *La Petite poule d'eau* (*Where Nests the Water Hen*), a pastoral novel set in an idyllic and isolated rural community in Northern Manitoba where Roy had once taught school for a summer. Such dramatic shifts of setting and subject matter became typical of her career which swung between two modes of vision, what the critic Hugo McPherson has called "the world of experience and the world of innocence." Particularly adept in the portrayal of strong female characters, she cannot be classified under any particular rubric. She wrote with compassion about Doukhobor, Ukrainian and Chinese immigrants, of Winnipeg slums and about the Arctic, of the clash of cultures between Inuits and whites, of an inhibited bank teller dying a slow death in Montreal.

Mark Abley cut to the heart of her talent when he wrote in *Maclean's* magazine, "Only a few modern writers, notably Isaac Bashevis Singer, could match her gift of portraying warmth without sentimentality, joy without delusion. Even when her work described alienation and loneliness, it also reached out in hope."

Excerpt from Gabrielle Roy's *Bonheur d'occasion*, translated by Hannah Josephson as *The Tin Flute*, (Toronto: McClelland & Stewart, 1947), 25-26.

The street was absolutely silent. There is nothing more peaceful than St. Ambroise Street on a winter night. From time to time a figure slips by, as if drawn to the feeble glimmer of a store front. A door opens, a square of light appears on the snow-covered street, and a voice rings out in the distance. The passerby is swallowed up, the door bangs shut, and only the spirit of the night reigns in the deserted street between the pale glow of lighted windows on one side and the dark walls bordering the canal on the other.

At one time the suburb had ended here; the last houses of Saint-Henri looked out on open fields, a limpid, bucolic air clinging to their eaves and tiny gardens. Of the good old days nothing is left now on St. Ambroise Street but two or three great trees that still thrust their roots down under the cement sidewalk. Mills, grain elevators, warehouses have sprung up in solid blocks in front of the wooden houses, robbing them of the breezes from the country, stifling them slowly. The houses are still there with their wrought-iron balconies and quiet facades. Sometimes music penetrates the closed shutters, breaking the silence like a voice from another era. They are lost islands to which the winds bear messages from all the continents, for the night is never too cold to carry over alien scents from the warehouses: smells of ground corn, cereals, rancid oil, molasses, peanuts, wheat dust and resinous pine.

Jean had chosen this remote, little-known street because the rent was low, and because the deep rumble of the quarter, the whistle blowing at the end of day, and the throbbing silence of the night spurred him on to work.

In the spring, to be sure, the nights ceased to be quiet. As soon as the channel was free of ice the sirens blew from sunset to dawn, echoing from the bottom of St. Ambroise Street over the entire suburb, and even as far as Mont-Royal when the wind blew that way.

SELECTED BIBLIOGRAPHY

Bonheur d'occasion (Montreal: Société des Éditions Pascal, 1945), translated by Hannah Josephson as *The Tin Flute*, (Toronto: McClelland & Stewart, 1947).

La Petite poule d'eau (Montreal: Beauchemin, 1950), translated by Harry Lorin Binsse as *Where Nests the Water Hen* (Toronto: McClelland & Stewart, 1952).

Alexandre Chenevert (Montreal: Beauchemin, 1954), translated by Harry Lorin Binsse as *The Cashier* (Toronto: McClelland & Stewart, 1955).

La Route d'Altamont (Montreal: HMH, 1966), translated by Joyce Marshall as *The Road Past Altamont* (Toronto: McClelland & Stewart, 1966).

Ces Enfants de ma vie (Montreal: Stanké, 1977), translated by Alan Brown as *Children of My Heart* (Toronto: McClelland & Stewart, 1979).

La Détresse et l'enchantement (Montreal: Boréal Express, 1984), translated by Patricia Claxton as *Enchantment and Sorrow: The Autobiography of Gabrielle Roy* (Toronto: Lester & Orpen Dennys, 1987).

HUGH MACLENNAN

Grand Old Man of Canadian Letters

ELSPETH CAMERON, Hugh MacLennan's biographer, dubbed him the "Grand Old Man of Canadian Letters." Yet though MacLennan spent a lifetime exploring the meaning of being Canadian in his novels and essays and virtually became a Canadian literary icon, he arrived at the subject through the back door at the suggestion of his American wife.

MacLennan's ambition had been to write a book about war and social change against an international backdrop in the style of Hemingway. He had already written two such novels and had had them rejected by publishers when his writer wife, Dorothy Duncan, advised him to pioneer a literature in which he represented Canadians not only to themselves but to the world outside.

"Why don't you put all this part of Nova Scotia in your next book?" she said during a summer trip to Nova Scotia. "Nobody's ever going to understand Canada until she evolves a literature of her own..."

The year was 1937. The Statute of Westminster recognizing Canada's political autonomy from Britain was a mere six years old. Ninety-eight per cent of books sold in Canada were still being imported from abroad.

In a spirit of experimentation, MacLennan, an impoverished schoolmaster at Lower Canada College in Montreal, began working on *Barometer Rising*, a tightly-knit novel about the tragic explosion that levelled Halifax in 1917. When it finally appeared in 1941, the book became a runaway success and established MacLennan on the course that would see him win international renown as well as five Governor General's Awards. (While the public knew him mainly as a novelist, critics judged him and Robertson Davies as the two best essayists in the country. Two of his prizes were for essay collections.)

An urbane Montrealer for most of his adult life, MacLennan (1907-90) was born in Cape Breton Island and always preserved a slight Gaelic lilt in his speech. His career as a student of classical Greek and Latin at Dalhousie, Oxford and Princeton was an act of duty to the driving demands of his unbending Presbyterian father, a doctor. (MacLennan pushed himself hard at all endeavours and to please his father also took up tennis, becoming a championship player.) But the influence of his musical, artistic mother showed up when he began to write romantic poetry as a Rhodes scholar at Oxford.

According to George Woodcock, MacLennan's classical studies transposed themselves to his fiction through a series of repeated Homeric symbols based on the *Odyssey*: the returning wanderer, the waiting woman, the fatherless child and the wise doctor. These symbolic figures recurred in settings and situations that were completely Canadian: the backwoods of New Brunswick, Cape Breton coal mining towns, sleepy Quebec villages, the streets of Montreal. His descriptions of the Canadian climate and countryside were the strongest features of his work.

More intelligent craftsman than inspired artist, MacLennan came to realize that "the novel is such an intimate form that you're stuck with your own country. If the country is not recognizable," he told Donald Cameron, "you have to try to make it so, in order to make your book intelligible."

The wild success of *Two Solitudes* when it appeared in 1945 (it was sold out by noon on the day the first reviews appeared) was attributable to both its timeliness in treating the conscription crisis of World War II and the sense of recognition it inspired in readers. MacLennan gave Canadians the first-time thrill of reading about conflict and coexistence between French and English on home turf and, in the initial euphoria of the book's publication, that sufficed.

Two Solitudes has not worn the test of time as well as *The Watch That*

Ends the Night, his most ambitious and most fully-realized novel. But by 1945 MacLennan felt a desperate need to quit his day job at Lower Canada College and rushed the work of revision that *Two Solitudes* still required. He succeeded in being financially independent for only six years, however. Before the days of Medicare, his wife's serious illness devoured his royalties and he was obliged to return to teaching. He became a professor of English at McGill and, to his surprise, fell in love with the university and its students. It was in the 1950s that he honed his skill as an essayist and wrote *The Watch That Ends the Night*, a work in which the national theme took a backseat to the demands of the story, to the book's distinct merit.

MacLennan was visited by both great success and great suffering in his life. Dorothy Duncan died in 1957, two years before the publication of *The Watch That Ends the Night*. In 1985, after thirty years of service to McGill, the university unceremoniously turned him out of his office space in the Arts Building. In his old age, his second wife was struck by lightning and suffered brain damage. He lived long enough to have successive generations of critics belittle his achievements.

But, for reflecting us back to ourselves at a time when to do so was an act of courage and daring, all of us—readers and writers alike—owe him a huge debt of gratitude.

Excerpt from Hugh MacLennan's *The Watch that Ends the Night* (Toronto: Macmillan, 1959), 4-5.

Powder snow lay deep and white on the slope of Mount Royal and was flecked with the foot and trail marks of the squirrels who lived on the mountain. On this clear winter evening after sunset there was a green blink in the sky, and as I looked up through the boles of the bare trees I saw a flash of bright colour and recognized a pheasant which also lived on the mountain and and survived the winters on scraps thrown to him out of apartment windows by old ladies who loved him. This pale twilight bathing the city erased time: it called me back to the Montreal which once had been one of the true winter cities of the world, with iced toboggan slides on the mountain and snow-shoers in scarlet sashes and tuques and gray homespuns bright against the snow and shacks with rank coffee and acrid air where you warmed your half-frozen feet in front of Quebec heaters and felt young and clean and untroubled. It was gone now that we were learning to live like New Yorkers. ...

We lived in the heart of Montreal but inside our apartment home it was always quiet and we never seemed conscious of the city. Nor is anything quite like the silence of a northern city at dawn on a winter morning. Occasionally there was a hiss or whisper and a brushing against the windows and I knew it was snow, but generally there was nothing but a throbbing stillness until the street cars began running up Côte-des-Neiges and I heard them as though they were winds blowing through old drains.

SELECTED BIBLIOGRAPHY

Barometer Rising (Toronto: Collins, 1941).
Two Solitudes (Toronto: Collins, 1945).
Each Man's Son (Toronto: Macmillan, 1951).
The Watch That Ends the Night (Toronto: Macmillan, 1959).
The Other Side of Hugh MacLennan: Selected Essays Old and New, edited by Elspeth Cameron (Toronto: Macmillan, 1978).

PART TWO

Epidemic Outbursts of Poetry and Fiction

GRATIEN GÉLINAS
Father of Quebec Theatre

"A CANADIAN PLAYWRIGHT MUST NOT IMITATE OTHERS," Gratien Gélinas once said. "He must write for himself, from his roots… Sentiment alone will not create a body of literature, a theatre. A literature expresses a nation which has found its personality. A man must marry—he needs children of his own, a family; fathers, brothers and relatives are not enough."

Gratien Gélinas is a quintessential father figure: at eighty-three, a silver haired and bearded pater familias of six, grandfather many times over, and a great-grandfather. When he began to act and write for radio in the 1930s, neither Quebec nor the rest of Canada had a dramatic tradition to call its own. Since then, Gélinas' stellar one man show as playwright, actor, director and stage-manager has been such a singular and inspiring performance that, in his own lifetime, he has been dubbed Father of the Quebec Theatre.

More than sixty years ago, when Gélinas first cast about for a living, he didn't have a hope of entry into the theatre. Born in St.-Tite de Champlain near Trois Rivières in 1909, he arrived in Montreal as a baby when his father, a saddle maker, was forced out of his trade by the advent of the car. From childhood, Gélinas had an affinity for the theatrical—his father was a born storyteller and his maternal uncles engaged in amateur theatricals, collecting exotic props and costumes that fascinated the little boy.

While a student at Collège de Montréal, Gélinas' teachers encouraged his dramatic flair, but the onset of the Depression obliged

him to quit school. He joined the accounting department of an insurance company, resolving to make of himself an amateur actor.
His ubiquitous appearances in local productions caught the attention of producers of the fledgling radio networks of the day, and in
1934 he won an important role in *Le Curé du village*, the first French-
Canadian radio serial. He turned professional.

His great chance came in 1937 when radio station CKAC offered
him $75 a week to write and perform a half-hour comedy.

Thus was born Fridolin, a home-grown Chaplinesque teenaged
hero. With his ever-present slingshot, moth-eaten Canadiens hockey
sweater, battered cap and filthy sneakers, Fridolin became an instant sensation. First Montreal, then the rest of the province, took
to its heart the street urchin who spoke the vernacular of the east
end, the first time a dramatic character had ever done so.

Fridolin became *Fridolinons* a stage revue in successive years from
1938-1946, going from strength to strength, as Gélinas' satire sharp-
ened and his characterizations deepened. It was slapstick, it was
situation comedy but it was, above all, *chez nous*. In 1946 alone,
performances were attended by more than 100,000 people in
Montreal and Quebec City, proving that—as Gélinas would later
write— "a play of Canadian inspiration and expression will always
grip our public more strongly than the greatest masterpieces of the
foreign theatre, past or present, however incomparable their dramatic value."

Two of the Fridolin skits— "Le Départ du conscrit" and "Le Retour
du conscrit"—formed the basis for Gélinas' first full-length play,
Tit-Coq, a landmark in the development of Quebec theatre. First
performed in 1948 with Gélinas in the lead, *Tit-Coq* united stage
with audience with an emotional punch that hit theatre-goers, both
French and English, with the blow of recognition.

Tit-Coq ("Little Rooster") is a slightly grown-up version of Fridolin,
an orphan and a bastard, about to be sent overseas in World War II,
a war he neither cares about nor understands. A fellow soldier takes
him home for Christmas and there Tit-Coq falls in love with his
buddy's sister, Marie-Ange. She reciprocates his feelings, but during his absence overseas marries someone else. Stormily reunited,
they plan to run off together until Tit-Coq's chaplain injects a dose

of reality into the scenario. Divorce is out of the question in the Quebec of the day; their children, like Tit-Coq, would be bastards. Heart-broken, Tit-Coq abandons his suit.

Forty-five years later, Tit-Coq's plight seems implausible. And in fact, after its remarkable local success (by 1951 it had played more than 500 performances in French and English in Montreal and then had a good run in Toronto), in its English version it flopped after three nights on Broadway. The New York audience could cope neither with the cast's Montreal-inflected English, nor with the melodramatic treatment of illegitimacy and divorce. Yet at home, it was precisely its ingrained domestic realism—the working-class ambience of war-time Montreal, the mirrored conflict between societal values and private passions, the colloquial idiom—that captivated the audience, validating its concerns as worthy of drama.

In *Bousille et les justes* (1959), his next play, Gélinas continued to plumb his Quebec roots but achieved a level of universality unique in his oeuvre. Bousille tells the story of a God-fearing simpleton who has unwittingly witnessed a murder and is tortured into perjury by his unscrupulous cousins in order to save the family honour. A tragicomedy which caricatures empty religiosity, Bousille pioneered theatre as social criticism in Quebec and, besides packing in audiences across the country, was adapted for television in Britain, Czechoslovakia, Finland and West Germany.

Besides writing, performing in and directing two other plays— *Hier les enfants dansaient* (1966), about the havoc wrought in a prominent Québécois family by a separatist son's terrorist plans, and *La Passion de Narcisse Mondoux* (1986), a romantic comedy— Gélinas has played Shakespeare at Stratford, acted in films and television, founded La Comédie Canadienne, and been chairman of the Canadian Film Development Corporation.

Pushing eighty, he performed *Narcisse Mondoux* with his wife Huguette Oligny more than 400 times across Canada and, for five and a half weeks played it in French and English on alternate nights off Broadway in New York. (Currently there are plans to remount the play.) Throughout his long, virtuoso career, he has been passionate in his commitment to both Quebec and Canada, sensitively portraying each to the other.

Excerpt from *Yesterday the ChildrenWere Dancing*, translated by Mavor Moore (Toronto and Vancouver: Clarke Irwin Publishing, 1967), 69-70. The speech is flung at Pierre Gravel who intends to run for office as a federal Liberal by Nicole, fiancée of André, Pierre's terrorist son.

NICOLE: Have you any idea what a colonial you are, even in your own home? ... An hour ago, on the phone, you were talking to your big boss, the Prime Minister of what you quiveringly call my beloved country. Had you felt the temptation, perfectly legitimate for a free man, to make him answer you in your mother tongue can you imagine how bewildered the poor dear great man would've been? And yet three out of ten of "his people" speak French. And Confederation is hardly a surprise—it's been around for a century! What's more a Nobel Prize winner isn't usually a dunce. So? He can't speak our language, or he won't speak it? Either way, you can kiss every finger of both his hands if you want to, but personally I say, "Nuts! Crap!"

SELECTED BIBLIOGRAPHY

Tit-Coq (Montreal: Beauchemin, 1950); translated by Kenneth Johnstone with the author, (Toronto: Clarke, Irwin, 1967).
Bousille et les justes (Quebec: Institut Littéraire du Québec, 1960); translated by Kenneth Johnstone and Joffre Miville-Dechêne as *Bousille and the Just*, (Toronto: Clarke, Irwin 1961).
Yesterday the Children Were Dancing, translated by Mavor Moore, (Toronto & Vancouver: Clarke, Irwin, 1967), original French version published as *Hier, les enfants dansaient* (Montreal: Leméac, 1968).

MONUMENT NATIONAL

MONTRÉAL

DU 22 AU 31 MAI 1948

Gratien Gélinas

présente

SA PIÈCE EN TROIS ACTES

"TIT-COQ"

•

Mise en scène:

GRATIEN GÉLINAS et FRED BARRY

•

Décors et éclairages:

JACQUES PELLETIER

•

Costumes:

LAURE CABANA

Programme for *Tit-Coq*, Montreal 1948

IRVING LAYTON
Happiest When Composing Poems

ISSIE LAZAROVITCH had a passion for the English language. Recalled a friend from his Baron-Byng-High-School days, "He would come into my place and throw a dictionary into my lap, saying 'Ask me any word! I know them all!' I'd try to catch him, but I never could. He did know the meaning of any word I picked."

Issie Lazarovitch tried out several names (Isadore Lazarre, Irving Lazarre, Pete Lazarovitch) and several occupations (Fuller Brush man and insurance salesman being the two most unsuitable) before he became Irving Layton and one of the great poets of the twentieth century. To his fellow poet Ralph Gustafson, Layton is one of only two Canadian poets who possessed "the Grand Style" (the other being A.M. Klein): grand both in content and in its "rolling, rhythmical syllabic music."

And Hugh MacLennan pronounced him "the best poet now producing steadily within the [English] language," when they both received Governor General's Awards in 1960 (MacLennan for his novel *The Watch That Ends the Night* and Layton for his collection *Red Carpet for the Sun*). In recognition for his achievements, among many other honours, Layton was nominated (by Italy and Korea) for the 1982 Nobel Prize (Canada nominated Josef Skvorecký).

Yet for all his fame—some would say notoriety—and his impressive literary output (some fifty books mostly of poetry, but also several volumes of correspondence and a memoir, *Waiting for the Messiah*), Layton the man casts a long shadow over his own writing. His flamboyance and bombastic utterances tend to deflect attention away from, instead of attracting readers to his work. Indeed, as Gustafson writes in his poem "Irving," "This man, grandiloquent/Boastful.../ Foolstruck,/In the glory of rage.../Like Joshua, commands/Contradictions."

It would be more surprising, perhaps, if he didn't.

Layton was the eighth and youngest child of Moishe and Keine Lazarovitch, an orthodox Jewish couple who arrived in Montreal from Romania in 1913 when Issie was a year old. "My father was an ineffectual visionary; he saw God's footprint in a cloud and lived only for his books and meditations." Otherworldly to the point that he no more noticed his children "than if we had been flies on the wall," Moishe died when his youngest was about twelve, as did an older brother near the same time.

Keine Lazarovitch, Layton's mother, made her children feel unwanted with the exception of Issie, the favourite who shared her bed till he was thirteen. The child had been born circumcised, a fact which his mother took to be a miraculous, even Messianic portent of greatness, a feeling she early transmitted to him.

Layton grew up in extreme poverty on St. Elizabeth Street in the east end. The front room of the family's four-room shack converted into the grocery store from which his mother eked out their living. In addition to resourcefulness, Keine "had a gift for cadenced vituperation; to which, doubtless, I owe my impeccable ear for rhythm," he wrote in the preface to *Red Carpet for the Sun*.

Despite the deprivation and the general unhappiness of his family life, it is noteworthy that two of Layton's richest and most affecting poems should be "Death of Moishe Lazarovitch" and "Keine Lazarovitch." And, in retrospect, he recalls the slums with fondness. "For a poet, nothing could have been better. Raw, vulgar, dynamic and dramatic, there were smells and sights and sounds and fights.... Sometimes I'm sorry for my children, who live in suburbs and never had anything like this."

While he wrote his first poem (inspired by the cleavage of his grade six teacher) when he was twelve, it was not readily apparent that Layton would become a poet till much later. He studied agriculture at Macdonald College, he divulges with a rollicking laugh in an interview in his Notre Dame de Grâce home, "because every student that came from Quebec got $9 per month: 7 times 9 is $63. The fee was $50 a year. I did some rapid mental arithmetic and realized I'd make a profit of $13. I couldn't resist." He later obtained an M.A. in Economics and Political Science from McGill.

Layton was nearly thirty when he met Louis Dudek at a lecture of the English Literary Society at McGill. Together "they were to be chemical elements that precipitated a cultural transformation," according to Layton's biographer, Elspeth Cameron.

Or, as Layton puts it more brutally, "When I began to write, no Canadian went to the bathroom or f——d."

Both Layton and Dudek agreed with the aims of the avant-garde poets writing in Montreal at the time—A.J.M. Smith, F.R. Scott and A.M. Klein among others—to energize the generally bloodless Canadian poetry of the day, but they mocked the discrepancy between the philosophy of the modernists and their actual works.

Eventually, Layton and Dudek joined forces with John Sutherland in the literary magazine *First Statement*. In the years ahead, Layton would gradually find the vital, ironic and often crude voice that has dazzled, puzzled and antagonized his readers. More than anyone else, he helped to dispel the puritanism and effeteness that stultified the Canadian literary scene in the 1940s and 1950s, and broke down barriers of subject, style and language.

Still writing after a career than spans nearly fifty years, in the next two years he will have twelve books appearing on three continents (his most recent collection is *Fornalutx: Selected Poems, 1928-1990* (McGill-Queen's Press, 1992). Layton's poetry reflects all facets of his bohemian life: his five wives (painter Betty Sutherland, his second wife—sister of John, the editor, and Donald, the actor—has written "we're almost numerous enough/your wives/to unionize") and assorted love affairs; his children; his mercurial political views (from a youthful flirtation with Communism to support of the Vietnam War and of the War Measures Act during the October Crisis of 1970, from forgiveness of Germany for the events of World War II to unqualified support for Israel); his friendships and feuds; his atheism and his Judaism.

Parallelling his writing, Layton has had a distinguished teaching career at Montreal's Herzliah High School, Jewish Public Library and Sir George Williams (later Concordia) University, and at York University in Toronto. Through charisma and energy (his teaching schedule included 18-hour days), he sparked a passion for poetry in his students, some of whom went on to write and many of whom became his friends.

The extravagance of his emotions and output—in large part the source of his success—has carried the seeds of his greatest flaws. When it comes to his own work, Layton seems unable to separate wheat from chaff and has often published in haste and overabundance. And the author of some of the most tender and eloquent love poems of our time ("So I envy the berries she puts in her mouth,/The red and succulent juice that stains her lips: I shall never taste that good to her"—"Berry Picking"), cannot grasp why his ideas as to women's limited horizons should offend and alienate many readers. ("Vision is strictly a man's prerogative,/So's creativity/Except for a handful of female freaks/With hair on their chins and enlarged glands" he wrote in *Lovers and Lesser Men* in 1973).

But, at his brilliant best, Layton's joy in creation ("and me happiest when I compose poems") becomes the reader's shared exhilaration.

"They dance best who dance with desire
Who lifting feet of fire from fire
Weave before they lie down
A red carpet for the sun."

"Keine Lazarovitch" excerpted from *A Wild Peculiar Joy* (Toronto: McClelland & Stewart, 1982), 86.

When I saw my mother's head on the cold pillow,
Her white waterfalling hair in the cheeks' hollows,
I thought, quietly circling my grief, of how
She had loved God but cursed extravagantly his creatures.

For her final mouth was not water but a curse,
  A small black hole, a black rent in the universe,
Which damned the green earth, stars and trees in its still-
ness
And the inescapable lousiness of growing old.

And I record she was comfortless, vituperative,
Ignorant, glad, and much else besides; I believe
She endlessly praised her black eyebrows, their thick weave,
Till plagiarizing Death leaned down and took them for his
mould.

And spoiled a dignity I shall not again find,
And the fury of her stubborn limited mind:
Now none will shake her amber beads and call God blind,
Or wear them upon a breast so radiantly.

O fierce she was, mean and unaccommodating;
But I think now of the toss of her gold earrings,
Their proud carnal assertion, and her youngest sings
While all the rivers of her red veins move into the sea.

SELECTED BIBLIOGRAPHY

A Red Carpet for the Sun (Toronto: McClelland & Stewart, 1959).
The Collected Poems of Irving Layton (Toronto: McClelland & Stewart, 1971).
A Wild Peculiar Joy: Selected Poems 1945-82 (Toronto: McClelland & Stewart, 1982).
Waiting for the Messiah: A Memoir (Toronto: McClelland & Stewart, 1985).
Fornalutx: Selected Poems, 1928-1990 (McGill-Queen's Press, 1992).

LOUIS DUDEK

Laureate of the Poets

"I want these poems to be where people are doing something,
not only among other poems in poetry magazines
but among stock quotations, ball scores, and the political squabble."
—LOUIS DUDEK, *Zembla's Rocks*

THE MAN WHO WROTE THESE LINES, who has all his life had "this obsession with the idea that poetry is so important"—as he told me in his
Lower Westmount living room—made his small gesture for bringing poetry into the hub of everyday Montreal by founding Poets'
Corner, a nook in Ben's Delicatessen hung with photographs of contemporary Canadian poets.

Not that Louis Dudek's poetry is alien to the pages of literary magazines. One of the most important contributors to the modern poetry movement in Canada, his work has appeared in little magazines—
several of which he founded or helped to found—for the last half
century. But despite a distinguished literary career as poet, professor, anthologist, critic, editor and publisher, few formal honours have
come Dudek's way. Modest and uninterested in self-promotion, he
has also been vocal in his opposition to art as competition and to the
divisive effects of prize-giving in the world of letters. ("He's more
interested in writing poetry ... and thinking about it, and writing
about it, than he is in any acclaim he might gather," fellow poet Ron
Everson once said of him.)

That's why the gesture of a group of Montreal writers to honour

Dudek at Poets' Corner in March 1990 was so fitting.

For more than thirty years as a teacher at McGill University and through his varied activities at the heart of the Montreal poetry scene, Dudek had a profound influence in nurturing emerging poets. (He published Leonard Cohen's first collection and his students included Daryl Hine, Seymour Mayne, Ken Norris, Raymond Filip and Sonja Skarstedt.) In an outpouring of affection and esteem, his disciples organized a day of overdue recognition for Dudek. They took up a collection to which some fifty Canadian writers from across the country contributed, presented him with the first "Canadian Writers' Award" at Ben's and organized a reading from his works at McGill.

Louis Dudek was born the second of three children, in Montreal in 1918. His parents were Polish immigrants—his father from Russia and his mother from England. The family lived modestly on Berczy Street in the east end of the city where his father, who spoke little English and no French, worked as a firefighter and truck driver.

A quiet, thoughtful child ("My childhood, apart from snow and rock fights with French Canadians and membership in the local gang of boys, was filled with reading novels of adventure, dozens of books from the local lending library and from a box of books stored in a back closet..." he told his biographer, Susan Stromberg-Stein), Dudek inherited his artistic sensibility from his mother who sang, played the piano and read avidly. Frail and sensitive, he was labelled a sickly child who was not likely to survive. This family judgement scarred him deeply, as did the early death of his mother when he was eight. He began writing poetry at about this time.

Despite his family's modest circumstances, money was found for him to attend McGill during the bitter years of the Depression. There, he worked on the *McGill Daily*—in which he published poems of social protest—and considered a career in journalism. After graduation, he found work as an advertising copywriter and took part in the city's lively poetry scene. He became one of the editors of the avant-garde, iconoclastic and anti-establishment little publication *First Statement* which, in 1945, merged with another literary magazine, *Preview*, to become *Northern Review*, then the largest and arguably most interesting literary magazine in the country. Its editors and contributors included John Sutherland, F.R. Scott, A.M. Klein, Irving

Layton, Ralph Gustafson, Dorothy Livesay, as well as Dudek. Discontented with the commercialized world in which he was making his living, Dudek enrolled at Columbia University in New York where he obtained a doctorate. He returned to Montreal to take up a teaching position at McGill in 1951, having been greatly influenced by the ideas of the American poet Ezra Pound with whom he had been in contact and correspondence in the United States. Convinced of the need for poets to take the publication of their works out of the hands of commercial publishing houses and into their own, Dudek became a major force in Canadian small-press publishing. He was one of the founders of Contact Press and of DC Books (which is still active in Montreal) and of the magazine *CIV/n*, and a major force in the McGill Poetry Series. For a number of years he printed his own magazine, *Delta*, in the basement of his house.

In addition to works of cultural and literary criticism, Dudek has published more than a dozen collections of poetry of exceptional range. His early poems were short and lyrical and imbued with social concern. His work of the 1950s and 1960s is regarded as breaking new ground in Canadian literature with the long poems *Europe*, *En Mexico* and *Atlantis*, where Dudek became the first Canadian poet to use open form in an extended work.

Sometimes criticized for didacticism and lack of emotion, Dudek's work has always been marked by intellectual toughness and a strong philosophical bent. His collections, *Zembla's Rocks* (1986) and *Small Perfect Things* (1991), show an energizing marriage of ideas and feeling that is a fitting rejoinder to his critics.

The poems in these two collections go back to the 1950s but have benefited from years of polishing since Dudek's retirement in 1984. Describing the poetic impulse to me, he was almost mystical.

The poems come unbidden as "gurgling spurts," he said. "It's not just realistic like here and now and practical. It's almost like a trance. It's from somewhere else and it's been given to you."

"A Warm Night," from *Zembla's Rocks* (Montreal: Véhicule Press, 1986), 31.

I walk in the warm wet night,

the streets glisten, the lights glimmer,
the air like chamois, night-soft with silence.
All things are possible,
The wind wraps a scarf around my middle—
o lift of sweet seduction.
There are dark corners,
lumps of black, diamonds of possibility,
and people storing their pain
in dark houses, with few windows, under the lit cross.

The city sleeps, while the night searches its hidden recesses,
                            with secret seed.
It leaves the city heavy with those deposits of daylight's progeny-
            whatever we do or dream.

I walk in the echoing streets searching
the opposites that meet, or trap the constellations
and the beautiful dark, in my net, as I lean
                    over the edge of night.

"The Classroom," from *Zembla's Rocks* (Montreal: Véhicule Press, 1986) 18.

When I saw the students coming in
with their warm, intelligent faces,
                    ready for another bout
with great ideas, analogies, interpretations, facts
                    and theories that always defeat us,
each of them independently fighting
                    for his own bit of ground
against embattled knowledge, against the karate of reason:
when I saw their patience, silence, meekness
before the imminent stream
        of accumulated lore, pouring down from glaciers
of unassuaged desire, the mountainous stupefactions of
tradition—
I sat down in pity, and held my head in my hands,
until love opened my eyes, and I bent listening to the chatter
                    of those enquiring minds.

SELECTED BIBLIOGRAPHY
With Irving Layton and Raymond Souster, *Cerberus* (Toronto: Contact, 1952).
Europe (Toronto: Contact, 1956).
En Mexico (Toronto: Contact, 1958).
Zembla's Rocks (Montreal: Véhicule, 1986).
Infinite Worlds: The Poetry of Louis Dudek, (Montreal: Véhicule, 1988).
Small Perfect Things (Montreal: DC Books, 1991).
Paradise: Essays on Myth, Art and Reality (Montreal: Véhicule 1992)

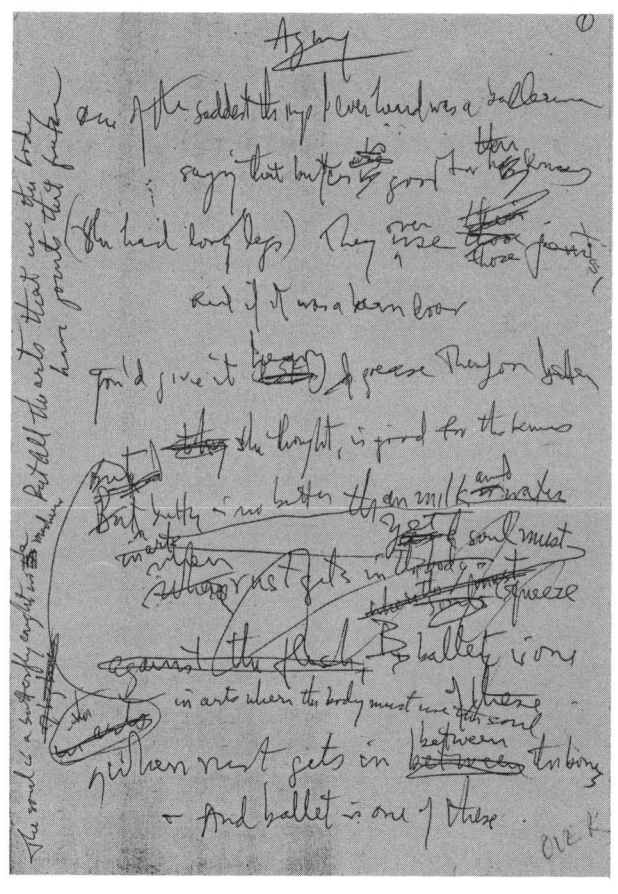

Manuscript page from work-in-progress by Louis Dudek.

117

MAVIS GALLANT
The Culture of Memory

"ONLY PERSONAL INDEPENDENCE MATTERS" was the epigraph to Mavis
Gallant's 1981 Governor General's Award-winning collection of short
stories about Canada, *Home Truths*. If four words can sum up a life,
these by Boris Pasternak, would be the ones to encapsulate Gallant's.

One of the finest living fiction writers of English, Gallant is a cosmopolitan self-exiled Canadian who thinks and dreams in English,
lives in French and has, for more than forty years (beginning in the
heyday of the Feminine Mystique), made her living by literature.
Always on her own stringent terms: no grants, no academic ties
(she didn't even go to university) and, with one exception, no writer-
in-residencies.

The personal and economic independence that Gallant has achieved,
by dint of sheer talent and grit, impress all the more in light of an
early life that might well have hobbled a less sturdy soul.

Mavis Young was born in 1922 in Montreal to parents who treated
her like "a mechanical doll." Her mother—daughter of a long line of
unmaternal women—"should not have had children," Gallant told
Barbara Gabriel in *The Canadian Forum* in 1985.

When she was four, her parents sent her to a French Catholic boarding school, a highly unusual step at that time for English Protestants
to take. Her mother promised to return and Mavis kept on waiting:
a sense of abandonment resonates in many a Gallant story and interview over the years.

Forbidden toys at the school, she was allowed to hold on to a book from home called *The Joyous Travellers*. "In those days—the nineteen twenties—it seemed to be mandatory for language teachers in both French and English schools in Canada to understand not a word of the language they set out to teach. The nun who taught English, and who might as well have been speaking Swahili for all I ever understood, held the book up to a class of docile little girls and announced that the title meant Les Joyeux Travailleurs, or The Happy Workers." When Mavis contradicted her, she was coerced into agreement by the withholding of food.

Her father died when she was ten; her mother soon remarried. By the time she had completed her schooling at eighteen, she had attended seventeen different schools in Quebec, Ontario, and the United States.

She returned to Montreal in 1940, determined to survive on her own. After a brief stint in the cutting room of the National Film Board, she obtained a job as features reporter for the *Montreal Standard*. She married John Gallant, a piano player from Winnipeg, whom she would shortly divorce.

In the meantime, Gallant was writing stories which she kept in a large picnic basket. In 1950, she took the plunge to full-time professional fiction writing. *The New Yorker* accepted the second story she sent them and paid her $600 at a time when she was making $50 a week. "It was a lot of money—I don't think I'd ever had $600 together, ever.... I thought it was $60," she told Janice Kulyk Keefer in an interview.

In pursuit of independence, Gallant left marriage, job and country. She tried Madrid, London and Rome before settling in Paris, a city she found congenial to the lifestyle of the single-woman writer. Yet she has maintained her Canadian citizenship and comes home on average twice a year.

"All lives are interesting; no one life is more interesting than another," Gallant has written in *Paris Notebook*, a book of essays. "Its fascination depends on how much is revealed, and in what manner." In over 100 short stories, which generally are published in the *New Yorker* before they appear in collections (she has also written two novels, two political studies and a play), Gallant writes about dislocation in time and place with masterful compression and restraint.

Her work is permeated with historical events and with politics whose shocks are seen and felt in the destructive personal relationships of her characters. Subversive laughter is perhaps her most devastating tool, chilly detachment the flaw for which critics most often chide her.

"I think the difference between a writer and everyone else is the ability to put yourself in someone else's place, completely," Gallant observed in an interview with Debra Martens in the now defunct Montreal literary magazine, *Rubicon*. Her many-layered stories of expatriates and Europeans convey both psychological and historical depth, with "the deeper culture" of memory intensifying resonances. Her own favourite among her books, *The Pegnitz Junction*, which deals with post-war Germany, explores the processes by which the past continues to haunt the present. The Linnet Muir stories, six interrelated loosely autobiographical stories in *Home Truths*, recreate in language of utter purity and economy a younger self from the point of view of a mature woman.

Such reductive summaries, however, can't do justice to Gallant's art. As Kildare Dobbs wrote in a 1979 review of *From the Fifteenth District* in *Saturday Night*, "She is one of those masters who achieve their effects with such seeming simplicity that we cannot see how it is done even when we know how it is done."

Excerpt from "With a Capital T," in *Home Truths* (Toronto: Macmillan of Canada, 1981, 317-318.

In wartime, in Montreal, I applied to work on a newspaper. Its name was *The Lantern*, and its motto, "My light shall shine," carried a Wesleyan ring of veracity and plain dealing. I chose it because I thought it was a place where I would be given a lot of different things to do. I said to the man who consented to see me, "But not the women's pages. Nothing like that." I was eighteen. He heard me out and suggested I come back at twenty-one, which was a soft way of getting rid of me. In the meantime I was to acquire experience; he did not say of what kind. On the stroke of twenty-one I returned and told my story to a different person. I was immediately accepted. I had expected to be. I still believed then, that most people meant what they said. I supposed that the man I had seen that first time had left a memorandum in the files: "To whom it may concern -Three years from this date, Miss Linnet Muir will join the editorial staff." But after I'd been working for a short time I heard one of the editors say, "If it hadn't been for the god-damned war we would never have hired even one of the god-damned women," and so I knew.

In the meantime I had acquired experience by getting married. I was no longer a Miss Muir, but a Mrs. Blanchard. My husband was overseas. I had longed for emancipation and independence, but I was learning that women's autonomy is like a small inheritance paid out a penny at a time. In a journal I kept I scrupulously noted everything that came into my head about this, and about God, and about politics. I took it for granted that our victory over Fascism would be followed by a sunburst of revolution - I thought that was what the war was about. I wondered if going to work for the capitalist press was entirely moral. "Whatever happens," I wrote, "it will be the Truth, nothing half-hearted, the truth with a Capital T."

SELECTED BIBLIOGRAPHY

The Pegnitz Junction: A Novella and Five Short Stories (Toronto: Macmillan, 1982).

From the Fifteenth District: A Novella and Eight Short Stories (Toronto: Macmillan, 1979).

Home Truths: Selected Canadian Stories (Toronto: Macmillan, 1981).

Overhead in a Balloon: Stories of Paris (Toronto: Macmillan, 1985).

Across the Bridge (Toronto: McClelland & Stewart 1993).

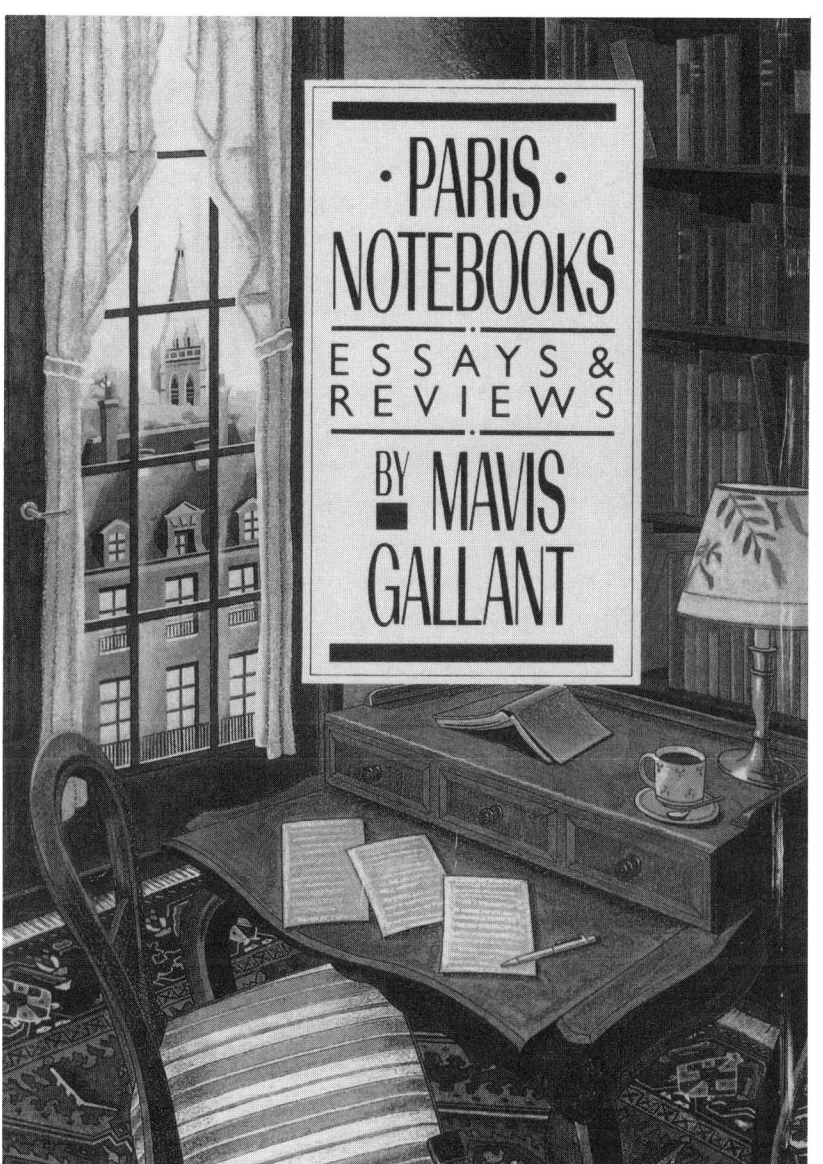

NAÏM KATTAN

Transcultural Canadian

HE HAS BEEN CALLED "OTTAWA'S GRANTS FAIRY" and "our only Arab-Jewish-French-Canadian writer." For nearly twenty-five years Naïm Kattan was the head of the Writing and Publication Section of the Canada Council. Today, as writer in residence at the Université du Québec à Montréal, he finally has the luxury of uninterrupted writing time, no longer obliged to rise at five in order to put in the dawn hours at the typewriter that have resulted in an oeuvre of some twenty books.

Kattan obtained his first office job in Iraq at the tender age of fourteen. But by then he was already a published author, his first story accepted by an Arabic literary magazine when he was still in short pants.

Kattan was born in Baghdad in 1928, the son of a Jewish minor civil servant and his wife. He was educated in an Alliance Israëlite Universelle school where, along with Arabic, his mother tongue, he learned Hebrew, French and English. Cosmopolitanism and duality are integral to his makeup.

Fiercely proud of twenty-five centuries of Jewish life in Babylon (the territory of modern-day Iraq), Iraqi Jews were nonetheless steeped in Arab culture and integrated into local society. In a recent interview Kattan spoke authoritatively of Iraq as the country of the Biblical patriarch Abraham, of the prophets Daniel and Ezra, the land where the Talmud was written. At the same time, he alluded to his youthful activities as an Arab nationalist. French became his adoptive language because, as a nascent Iraqi nationalist, he associated the English language with the colonial power that, in Iraq, was British.

The vicious World-War-II Iraqi pogrom known as the Farhoud and Iraq's subsequent implacable opposition to the existence of the state of Israel sent Kattan, like the vast majority of Iraqi Jews, into exile. He won a scholarship to the Sorbonne and lived in Paris for seven years. In 1954 he emigrated to North America and settled in Montreal.

In the closed-in, overwhelmingly Catholic society of the day, "I was an exquisite oddity," Kattan recalled. "A French-speaking Jew from Iraq... I spent the first two months without working and almost without eating." But, paradoxically, he also found his new country full of promise and opportunity. Working at first for the Canadian Jewish Congress and later as a literary critic for *Le Devoir*, his mission came to be the reflecting back to each other of Canada's solitudes.

He founded the *Bulletin du Cercle Juif* which had as its aim the creation of contacts between French Canadians and Jews. He married actress Gaétane Laniel (from whom he is now separated), wrote for *Cité Libre*, rubbed shoulders with people on the cusp of of attaining influence and power: René Lévesque, Pierre Trudeau, André Laurendeau. The last named, then editor of *Le Devoir*, commissioned him to write on the subject of English-Canadian literature. These articles became the basis for Kattan's wide-ranging three-volume collection of literary criticism on the literatures of the United States, English Canada and Latin America, *Écrivains des Amériques (1972-80)*.

A gap of nearly twenty years separates the end of Kattan's writings in Arabic and the beginning of his career as a writer of essays, short stories and novels in French. When he came to Canada, he consciously decided to stop writing in his native language because of the lack of a market, but the effort of switching to French for creative work cost him years of productivity.

When he did begin to publish, his writing was immediately acclaimed in the French press, and his first three books were almost simultaneously translated into English. His first essay collection, *Le Réel et le Théâtral* (1970) (translated as *Reality and Theatre*), combined autobiography with philosophical speculation about different perceptions of reality in Eastern and Western thought, culture and language—and won the France-Canada Award. In it he wondered, "Can I preserve the East without reducing it to exoticism or nostalgia? Can I accept the West without making into an ethic my fears of the dangers it contains, without making a moral principle of my resistance to annihilation?"

Kattan's honours include the J.I. Segal prize, the Order of Quebec, the Order of Canada and the Order of Arts and Letters of the French government.

His two early autobiographical novels, *Adieu, Babylone* (1975, translated as *Farewell, Babylon*) and *Les Fruits Arrachées* (1977, translated as *Paris Interlude*), recount the story of a young Iraqi Jew first in Baghdad during World War II, then in post-war Paris.

Kattan alternates between works of fiction and non-fiction. He has, for instance, recently followed up his 1991 novel *Farrida*, the story of a Jewish woman struggling to become a singer in the Baghdad of the 1930s, with *La Reconciliation*, an essay collection exploring the tension between the individual and society. Future projects include a novel for young people about the life of poet A.M. Klein, and a major study of the global relationship between cultures. In all his books, Kattan explores culture shock and the confrontation between occident and orient, male and female, Jew and Arab, Arabic and French.

Kattan's elliptical style is derived from Arabic narrative techniques. Quite often, essential details are left unsaid and result in a mysterious and lean account that hints at many layers of meaning. Critic William French has written of his work: "His range of knowledge, his choice of subjects and setting and his often challenging style establish him as a fiction writer quite unlike anyone else in this country."

Excerpt from *Adieu, Babylon*, translated by Sheila Fischman as *Farewell, Babylon* (Toronto: McClelland & Stewart, 1976), 65-66.

The next day after school I went to the offices of the magazine. I wandered cautiously through the unfamiliar streets in the heart of the Muslim section. The fear of the Jew moving through enemy territory was mixed with the emotion I felt at the coming confrontation with the great writer.

I found myself in the red-light district. Impelled by a powerful curiosity, I automatically slowed down. In this place of perdition my nascent virility made me forget my fear. These women had all the attractions I had dreamed about. I had only to cross the street. They were no longer part of the world of dream and imagination. Would I dare to cross the threshold? Two policemen standing at the door searched every visitor. Anyone with a dagger or a revolver who had come to wash his stained honour had to be kept aside. Until they slit the throat of the offending woman, whether sister, daughter or cousin, they would be covered with disgrace. So pressing was my desire to be initiated into manhood before seeing the editor-in-chief that I hardly trusted myself to cross the guarded doorway alone. But my short pants gave me a good argument to get out of the situation.

The magazine office and the editor's house were in the same building. I knocked at the door. A little girl opened it. I uttered the name of the master. The child could not take her eyes off me. Without moving she shouted, "Baba, a boy wants to see you."

"Tell him to come up."

SELECTED BIBLIOGRAPHY

Le Réel et le Théâtral (Montreal: HMH, 1970); translated by Alan Brown as *Reality and Theatre* (Toronto: Anansi, 1972).

Écrivains des Amériques, 3 volumes (Montreal: Hurtubise HMH, 1972-80).

Adieu, Babylone (Montreal: La Presse, 1975); translated by Sheila Fischman as *Farewell, Babylon* (Toronto: McClelland & Stewart, 1976).

Les Fruits Arrachées (Montreal: Hurtubise HMH, 1977); translated by Sheila Fischman as *Paris Interlude* (Toronto: McClelland & Stewart, 1979).

The Neighbour and Other Stories, translated, from a variety of Kattan's short-story collections, by Judith Madley and Patricia Claxton (Toronto: McClelland & Stewart, 1982).

René Levesque

Naïm Kattan

Nous sommes en 1954. Le Devoir venait de publier la traduction par Gilles Marcotte d'un article que j'avais publié en anglais sur le roman d'Yves Thériault : Aaron. On m'appelle au téléphone : " Mon nom est René Levesque. Nous consacrons demain notre émission radiophonique Carrefour à Yves Thériault et nous voudrions vous interviewer." C'était m█████████ière émission à Montréal. Un homme a██████████████ la voix cassée m'accueille. █████████████████████████ée, plus grande que █████████████████████████████s avons huit minu█████████████████████████████par les deux mais ████████████████████████████ns directes, incisive ██████████████████████████endais bien compte █████████████████████████████ipé à des émissions██████████████████████████t ce style me parais.██████████████████████████quais de passer à l█████████████████████████onie. Il dirigeait l'o█████████████████████████ela ne me choquai██████████████████████████J'étais fasciné par ████████████████████████s le chuchottement.███████████████████████████anti- radiophonique █████████████████████████ais content d'être ████████████████████████uc l'essentiel.

Typescript and original 'steno pad' manuscript
by Naïm Kattan

HUGH HOOD

Faith and Ambition

HUGH HOOD HAS BEEN HAILED as Canada's best short story writer—
"one of the five or six best short story writers now alive in the English-speaking world," according to critic John Mills writing in *The
Fiddlehead*. Robert Fulford dubbed him—in his guise of creator of a
projected twelve-volume novel series chronicling 20th-century Canadian life (now more than half-way completed)—"the begetter of
the most ambitious fictional project in the history of Canadian letters." A reviewer of his most recent short story collection, *You'll
Catch Your Death* referred to Hood as "an old master ... completely in
touch with today."

Despite these accolades, Hood is hardly a literary household word.
While he has published nearly thirty volumes of essays, biography
and criticism as well as the fiction upon which his reputation largely
rests, his writings do not attract the wide readership of an Atwood, a
Munro, or a Davies.

Erudite and intellectual—he has described himself as "somewhere
between a realist and a transcendental allegorist"—he has nonetheless shown an abiding interest in popular culture, writing about fash-
ion, baseball and hockey (including a biography of Jean Béliveau).
His fiction has appeared in both small liteary magazines and *Esquire*
and *Saturday Night*.

In a 1983 interview with Geoff Hancock in *Books in Canada,* Hood
visualized his ideal reader as a "person who enjoys the music of Joseph

131

Haydn better than anyone else…, the fully mature, well-educated, highly intelligent person of either sex, probably a Jew or a Christian… But it would help if the reader was interested in Christian personalism, Munier, Maritain, and others. And Flannery O'Connor."

Not perhaps the most hail-fellow-well-met sort of invitation to a prospective reader. But Hood has not been one to court readers or publicity. Calling the *Montreal Gazette* an "anti-religious, an anti-Christian newspaper," he refused to be interviewed by me when I originally researched this essay for the newspaper.

Key to even an elementary appreciation of Hood's art is his staunch Catholicism. Weaned on the Scriptures and educated in Catholic schools, he has described himself as "through and through a Catholic" writer, and sincerely searches in ordinary daily life for evidence of a higher meaning. "Human art and love are models of immortality," states the epigraph to one of his books.

Hood was born in Toronto in 1928 to parents who embodied Canada's linguistic duality. His father was an anglophone from Nova Scotia; his mother, French-Canadian by extraction, grew up in one of the earliest French communities of Toronto. (One of his short stories, "Brother André, Père Lamarche and My Grandmother Eugénie Blagdon," powerfully evokes his grandmother, once "a great strong solid heavy-jawed obstinate girl" who, at ninety-two, "still had some brown hair, the big strong stubborn jaw, and the terrible French-Canadian pertinacity.")

Hood, who has spent most of his life in Toronto and Montreal (he now lives in the Notre Dame de Grâce district of Montreal), has remained faithful to his bicultural roots: since 1961 he has taught English literature at the Université de Montréal. In 1964, with typical ambitiousness, he wrote to *Le Devoir* literary critic Naïm Kattan that he wanted to unite in his novels and stories "la totalité de notre culture, la culture la plus intéressante du monde."

Flying a Red Kite (1962), his first collection of stories, consisted of eleven pieces that included both works of allegory and documentary realism. Rich in literary and biblical allusions, these stories appeared to puzzle the critics (some of whom damned him with faint praise for his "chic *Esquire* English," and convincing portrayals of Canadians in "specific Canadian situations").

Two novels which followed—*White Figure, White Ground* (1964) and *The Camera Always Lies* (1967)—concerned the search for artistic integrity, in the former by a Nova Scotia painter, in the latter by a Hollywood actress. In each, Hood displayed what would become a trademark trait: a convincing knowledge of the technical aspects of his characters' jobs.

One of the original members of the Montreal StoryTellers performance group (along with John Metcalf, Clark Blaise, Ray Smith and Ray Fraser; the two Rays and Hood sharing a love of touch football as well as of literature), Hood frequently read his stories in Montreal high schools, community colleges and universities in the early and mid-1970s.

His notable short-story collections include *Around the Mountain: Scenes from Montreal Life* (1967), a collection in which the boundary between fiction and essay is provocatively blurred; *The Fruit Man, The Meat Man & The Manager* (1971) and *None Genuine Without This Signature* (1980).

With The New Age/Le Nouveau Siècle series begun some twenty years ago with *The Swing in the Garden* (of which to date eight volumes have appeared), Hood has set out to express nothing less than a fictional representation of the total Canadian experience in this century. Critics argue as to whether he is Proustian, as he claims, or "merely" Balzacian: whether his fictional world unfolds through the patient accretion of detail or through the power of imagination.

Either way, Hood has set himself a task as noble as it is unrealizable. As he has written in the 1980 essay "Trusting the Tale," "I'd like to hit every imaginable reader … with maximum artisitic force…, to coax them on the printed page into fascinated reading after reading. To make them applaud and make them meditate and finally pray."

Excerpt from "The Holy Man," in *The Fruit Man, The Meat Man & the Manager* (Ottawa: Oberon, 1971), 115-6. The story describes the evolution of Menahem Luboshutz, a young Jewish boy, from poet to saint.

I don't know what to say about his miracles, not actually having witnessed any. Perhaps I should ignore the whole matter but I don't think so. Being a Christian, I believe in miracles, and I've even given the question of defining them a certain amount of thought, but I won't advance a definition. I simply observe that sometimes—rarely—the customary order of nature is interrupted; the lame walk, the blind see and the deaf hear. The man who is persuaded that every such event must have a hidden natural and discoverable cause hasn't got me on his side. Some things happen that are difficult to understand, and not just on the lines of physical cures either. Some of the people around Menahem Luboshutz were transformed more remarkably in their hearts than in their bodies. He made the cruel sometimes kind. People changed their lives at his entreaty. This is miraculous.

There were plenty of physical wonders, especially cures. I have heard from her friends that a child sick eight years of polio recovered the use of her limbs in his presence, and that a leukemia went into prompt remission and stayed there when he commanded it. I have never heard of disreputable tricks—levitation and the like. The stories are chaste and sane, credible, but nevertheless miraculous. Nothing of the magician or the charlatan, everything of the saint. On all the streets of the area he became a byword, and over the last four years his reputation has filtered west to De Vimy, where I live, and further, carried along the Van Horne bus line out to Hampstead and from there to Côte Saint Luc, until by now he's famous all over the city.

SELECTED BIBLIOGRAPHY

Flying a Red Kite (Toronto: Ryerson, 1962).

Around the Mountain: Scenes from Montreal Life (Toronto: Peter Martin Associates, 1967).

The Fruit Man, The Meat Man & The Manager (Ottawa: Oberon, 1971).

None Genuine Without This Signature (Downsview, Ontario: ECW 1980).

The Swing in the Garden, (Ottawa: Oberon, 1975).

MORDECAI RICHLER
Écrivain Provocateur

ONE OF CANADA'S MOST OUTSPOKEN WRITERS, Mordecai Richler is probably the best-known author Montreal has ever spawned. Caustic,
controversial and often crude, he shares with the title character of his
most recent novel, *Solomon Gursky Was Here*, "an unquenchable itch to
meddle and provoke."

But Richler's acerbic and scatological inventiveness is fired by a
secular moralism that is less obvious, though no less important, to an
appreciation of his work than is his gleeful obscenity.

"In a time when there really is no agreement on values," he once
observed to Tom Harpur, the religion columnist of the *Toronto Star*,
"and a collapse of religious values, which certainly created a certain
order, or standard, you are obliged to work out your own code of
honour and system of beliefs and to lead as honourable a life as possible."

For Richler, "the honourable life" appears to have meant being a
devoted husband and loving father to his family of five grown children (his oldest son, Daniel, a child of his wife's first marriage, is also
a novelist and television arts critic)—and of writing precisely as he
pleases. Stupidity, hypocrisy, pretentiousness and greed have always
been the cardinal sins in his canon, targets of the savage wit that is as
acidic and uproarious today as it was when he began to write nearly
forty years ago.

Raised in an orthodox Jewish setting in the ghetto of Montreal
during the Depression ("where you could take in three movies for a

quarter, but sometimes felt gray squishy things nibbling at your ankles"), on his mother's side the grandson of a scholarly rabbi, since the publication of his first novel in 1954 Richler has grappled with the same themes: "Man without God. Man embarrassed. Stripped. There is a current chaos in the world, and we no longer know what is right or wrong."

He was born in 1931, the second son of an ill-matched couple. His father dealt in scrap metal and has been described by Philip Marchand in *Chatelaine* as "a chronic loser"; his mother, Leah Rosenberg, had certain literary pretensions of her own and, in 1981, produced a memoir entitled, *The Errand Runner: Reflections of a Rabbi's Daughter*. The family lived on St. Urbain Street till Mordecai was thirteen, when his parents separated. Though he left Canada at nineteen to spend nearly twenty years in Europe and now divides his time between an apartment in Montreal and a house in the Eastern Townships, he has written that he feels "forever rooted in Montreal's St. Urbain Street. That was my time, my place, and I have elected myself to get it right."

Robert Fulford has called Baron Byng High School, immortalized in *The Apprenticeship of Duddy Kravitz*, *St. Urbain's Horseman* and *Joshua Then and Now* as Fletcher's Field High School, Richler's Yoknapatawpha County. (When Richler was there, though, it was no immortal haunt. Said Saidye Bronfman, widow of the distillery magnate Sam Bronfman, patronizingly to Richler at the 1974 premiere of the movie version of Duddy Kravitz, "You've come a long way for a St. Urbain Street boy." Retorted Richler, "You've come a long way for a bootlegger's wife.")

Duddy Kravitz (1959) was his fourth novel and the one in which for the first time "I really came up with an original work drawn from my own real experience." Despite the ambitious scope of *Solomon Gursky*, the compassionate affirmation of *St. Urbain's Horseman* and the craftsmanship of *Joshua Then and Now*, *Duddy Kravitz* remains the best-known of Richler's works. A comic extravaganza of a coming-of-age novel, it tells the story of a "scheming little bastard," a coarse, driven, young Jew determined to make something of himself at any cost. A critical success both in Canada and beyond, the book inspired a raging controversy and denunciations by the Jewish community that Richler was an anti-Semite.

Richler himself has said, "I'm much more interested in criticizing, always, the things I believe in or I'm attached to, which may be a very perverse kind of love, but it's the only kind I'm capable of." That twenty-year-old interview with Donald Cameron is perhaps the best rejoinder to the latest Richlerian debate over his most recent book, *Oh Canada! O Quebec!*, in which he denounces, among other things, the anti-Semitic strain in French-Canadian nationalism. (In a recent telephone interview, however, Richler would only comment, "As far as the Quebec book goes, I really don't understand what all the furor is about. All I did was lay things out the way things were.")

The fate of the Jews, in particular during the Holocaust, is an abiding leitmotif in Richler's work: his heroes are frequently successful men haunted by their relatively easy ride through life, too young to fight in the War, and sheltered from the horrors that afflicted fellow Jews in Europe.

Brief stints as writer-in-residence aside, Richler is one of a minority of Canadian writers to make a successful living exclusively by the pen. Unassumingly labelling himself a freelancer, he has written for television and film, and, in between the novels that have become increasingly more laborious for him to craft (five years for *Horseman*, nearly a decade each for *Joshua* and *Solomon Gursky*), produced an impressive body of essays, reviews, anthologies and two highly popular children's books.

Critical response to his work has probably been affected by his curmudgeonliness and his lambasting of Canadian cultural nationalism. He has won two Governor General Awards for his early work (a joint prize for the novel *Cocksure* and the essay collection *Hunting Tigers under Glass* in 1968, and the fiction prize for *St. Urbain's Horseman* in 1971). *Solomon Gursky*, which was glowingly reviewed in the *New York Times*, touted for a Booker Prize in Britain and won the $20,000 Commonwealth Writers Prize as best fiction for 1990, was not even nominated for a Governor General's Award at home. In Quebec, however, the book received the QSPELL fiction prize.

Critics charge him with repeating himself, with creating stick female characters and of being unable to pull off a credible sex scene. Yet even the most scathing among them concedes that "his prose is

lively, he writes nervy dialogue, he has imaginative flair."
But no critic is as hard on him as is Richler himself.
"Each novel is a failure, or there would be no compulsion to begin afresh."

Excerpt from *St. Urbain's Horseman* (Toronto: McClelland & Stewart, 1971), 396-397. Jake Hersh returns to Montreal from England for the funeral and week of mourning for his father.

Sitting with the Hershes, day and night, a bottle of Remy Martin parked between his feet, such was Jake's astonishment, commingled with pleasure, in their responses, that he could not properly mourn for his father. He felt cradled, not deprived. He also felt like Rip Van Winkle returned to an innocent and ordered world he had mistakenly believed long extinct. Where God watched over all, doing His sums. Where everything fit. Even the holocaust which, after all, had yielded the state of Israel. Where to say, "Gentlemen, the Queen," was to offer the obligatory toast to Elizabeth II at an affair, not to begin a discussion on Andy Warhol. Where smack was not habit forming but what a disrespectful child deserved; pot was what you simmered the chicken soup in; and camp was where you sent the boys for the summer. It was astounding, Jake was incredulous, that after so many years and fevers, after Dachau, after Hiroshima, revolution, rockets in space, DNA, bestiality in the streets, assassinations in and out of season, there were still brides with shining faces who were married in white gowns, posing for the *Star* social pages with their prizes, pear-shaped boys in evening clothes. There were aunts who sold raffles and uncles who swore by the *Reader's Digest*. French Canadians, like overflying airplanes distorting the TV picture, were only tolerated. DO NOT ADJUST YOUR SET, THE TROUBLE IS TEMPORARY. Aunts still phoned each other every morning to say what sort of cake they were baking. Who had passed this exam, who had survived the operation. A scandal was when a first cousin was invited to the bar mitzvah kiddush, but not the dinner. Eloquence was the rabbi's sermon. They were ignorant of the arts, they were overdressed, they were overstuffed, and their taste was appallingly bad. But within their self-contained world, there was order. It worked.

SELECTED BIBLIOGRAPHY

The Apprenticeship of Duddy Kravitz (London: Deutsch, 1959).
St. Urbain's Horseman (Toronto: McClelland & Stewart, 1971).
Home Sweet Home: My Canadian Album (Toronto: McClelland & Stewart, 1984).
Solomon Gursky Was Here (Markham: Viking, 1989).
Broadsides: Reviews and Opinions (Markham: Viking,1990).

SUZANNE

Words and Music by LEONARD COHEN

PROJECT SEVEN MUSIC, a division of C.T.M.P. Inc.
515 Madison Ave., Suite 2207, New York, N. Y. 10022

LEONARD COHEN

Erotic Mystic, Apocalyptic Troubador

HE GREW UP IN WESTMOUNT, aspired to be a forest ranger as a child and became one of the best-known singer-songwriters of the late twentieth century. His international acclaim as a pop star has by now largely obscured his earlier writing career. But, before his gravelly croak ever assaulted the ear, Leonard Cohen had written *Beautiful Losers* (1966)—one of the most daring experimental novels in Canadian letters. (Desmond Pacey called it "the most intricate, erudite and fascinating Canadian novel ever written.") It has sold more than three million copies and been translated into twenty languages.

Cohen's *Selected Poems: 1956-1968* sold out its first printing of a quarter of a million copies in a few months, an astonishing achievement in poetry sales. It also won the 1969 Governor General's Award for its author, who turned the prize down.

The *New York Times* has called Leonard Cohen "a kind of rock and roll Lord Byron" and pronounced his penultimate album, *I'm Your Man*, "a masterpiece, pure and by no means simple." A recent profile in *Saturday Night* magazine by Ian Pearson characterized him as a "poet, an apocalyptic lounge lizard, a committed Jew, a disciplined Zen devotee, a madman in the recording studio, a blocked songwriter prone to breakdowns, a devoted father, an incorrigible ladies' man, and the happy companion of a beautiful young actress" (Rebecca De Mornay). But despite the reams written about him in the popular press and a voluminous biography (*Leonard Cohen: Prophet of the Heart* by Loranne Dorman and Clive Rawlins, Omnibus 1990), Cohen remains both elusive and mysterious, easier to access through his work than by what has been written about him.

He was born in 1934 in Montreal, the second child of Masha Klinitsky, a nurse, and Nathan Cohen, a wealthy clothing manufacturer. His mother, the daughter of a rabbi, immigrated to Canada with her family as refugees from Poland in the 1920s. His paternal grandfather, Lyon Cohen, was a prominent leader of the Jewish community who founded Montreal's *Jewish Times* which would later be absorbed by the *Canadian Jewish Chronicle*.

Despite an economically privileged childhood, tragedy touched Cohen early in life. His father, a semi-invalid as a result of injuries suffered in World War I, died when Leonard was nine. Thirteen years later, the young poet would dedicate *Let Us Compare Mythologies*, his first book of poems, "To the memory of my father."

At McGill he studied with Hugh MacLennan and Louis Dudek (who published *Let Us Compare Mythologies*), at the same time forging a life-long friendship with Irving Layton, who had a deep influence on him. They remain steadfast friends, Layton portraying him in *Saturday Night* as both saint and hedonist. Indeed, religion, sex, death, violence, beauty and the search for ecstasy have been the touchstones of his work from the beginning and continue to fascinate him in his newest recording, the apocalyptic *Future*.

Cohen's most prolific writing period was the 1960s during which he published four volumes of poetry, two novels and launched his first recording. He continues to write poetry even now, albeit slowly, and a new collection, *Stranger Music: Selected Poems and Songs*, is projected for publication in the fall of 1993. He works with painful and perfectionistic obsessiveness, the words torn out of him. ("I've had to scrape them out of my heart," he has said.)

Montreal, Cohen's "'Jerusalem of the North,' ... a holy city" where "the spirit was somehow invigorated" has been an all-important inspiration from the earliest poems such as "Saint Catherine Street" and "Had We Nothing to Prove" in *Let Us Compare Mythologies*; through his first published novel, *The Favourite Game* (1963), a semi-autobiographical account of a Montreal Jewish boy who finds his vocation as a poet; through *Beautiful Losers*, one of whose main characters is the Mohawk Indian saint Catherine Tekakwitha; and through many of his songs, such as "Suzanne Takes You Down" (which Douglas Barbour has called the most beautiful song of a whole generation). Cohen still maintains a residence in the core of the city (off Boulevard St. Laurent) and returns frequently from Los Angeles.

In a recent interview, Louis Dudek with deadpan wit described a turning point in Cohen's career from writer to singer-composer. The setting: F.R. Scott's Westmount home where Montreal's literati gathered frequently in the 1960s and where that night guests included Al Purdy and Dudek as well as Cohen.

"'Are you people still writing that same-old fashioned poetry?'" Dudek recalls Cohen addressing the gathering. "'Bob Dylan is the most important poet now in America!' And Frank Scott ran out and bought (Dylan's) record. And we all played it and we all thought it was crap. Especially Al Purdy."

For Dudek, a rigorous aestheticist and long-ago mentor to Cohen, the words of songs can never rank as serious poetry. "When the music takes over," says Dudek, "it carries all the feeling. And tone is carried by the melody and the rhythm. So what the hell, you don't need to say much!"

But for Cohen, there is nothing antithetical about poetry and song. He told a pair of interviewers in 1984, "It's just a different mode. There is something about reading lines on a page which is very powerful. Hearing something also has its powers. I wouldn't set up a conflict between forms."

And so Montreal's dark voluptuary (whose eclectic awards now include an honorary degree from McGill University, Officer of the Order of Canada, a Governor General's Performing Arts Award, and membership in the Juno Hall of Fame) will continue to seduce with the sensuousness of his language, haunt with his ominous vision and alternately inspire and outrage with his wild iconoclasm.

Excerpt from *Beautiful Losers* (Toronto: McClelland & Stewart, 1966), 3-4.

Catherine Tekakwitha, who are you? Are you (1656-1680)?

Is that enough? Are you the Iroquois Virgin? Are you the Lily of the Shores of the Mohawk River? Can I love you in my own way? I am an old scholar, better-looking now than when I was young. That's what sitting on your ass does to your face. I've come after you, Catherine Tekakwitha. I want to know what goes on under that rosy blanket. Do I have any right? I fell in love with a religious picture of you. You were standing among birch trees, my favorite trees. God knows how far up your moccasins were laced. There was a river behind you, no doubt the Mohawk River. Two birds in the foreground would be delighted if you tickled their white throats or even if you used them as an example of something or other in a parable. Do I have any right to come after you with my dusty mind full of the junk of maybe five thousand books? I hardly even get out to the country very often. Could you teach me about leaves? Do you know anything about narcotic mushrooms? Lady Marilyn just died a few years ago. May I say that some old scholar four hundred years from now, maybe of my own blood, will come after her in the way I come after you? But right now you must know more about heaven. Does it look like one of these little plastic altars that glow in the dark? I swear I won't mind if it does. Are the stars tiny, after all? Can an old scholar find love at last and stop having to pull himself off every night so he can get to sleep? I don't even hate books any more. I've forgotten most of what I've read and, frankly, it never seemed very important to me or to the world.

SELECTED BIBLIOGRAPHY

The Spice-Box of Earth (Toronto: McClelland & Stewart, 1961).
Flowers for Hitler (Toronto: McClelland & Stewart, 1964).
Beautiful Losers (Toronto: McClelland & Stewart, 1966).
Selected Poems, 1956-1968 (Toronto: McClelland & Stewart, 1968).
Book of Mercy (Toronto: McClelland & Stewart, 1984).
Stranger Music: Selected Poems and Songs (Toronto: McClelland & Stewart, 1993).

ROCH CARRIER

Fabulous Fabulist

ROCH CARRIER is probably English Canada's most widely-read contemporary francophone writer, author of the children's classic *The
Hockey Sweater* and the whimsically profound *Prayers of a Very Wise
Child* for which he won the 1992 Stephen Leacock Memorial Medal
for Humour. But Carrier, a writer for more than thirty years, has a
very broad range. Alongside his recent children's titles—*The Boxing
Champion*, *Happy New Year's Day* and *Canada, Je t'Aime / I Love You*—
stand *Fin*, a study of the suicide of a sixtyish engineer ironically named
Victor Joyeux, and the newly-translated *Man in the Closet*, a dreamy
mock-thriller which probes beneath the skin of rape and murder.

Carrier's vision is paradoxical: violence, mutilation and acciden-
tal death frequent his rollicking tales, plays and novels. With a steady
output of about a book a year, he defies easy categorization. Novelist, playwright, scriptwriter, professor, theatre administrator, chairman for several years of Montreal's Salon du Livre, rector of Collège
militaire royal de St-Jean (his current day job), Carrier's resumé is
long and impressive. His singular blend of fantastical allegory, dark
satire and social realism centred on rural Quebec has won him many
awards, including the Prix de Québec in 1964 for his first short story
collection, the Grand Prix Littéraire de la Ville de Montréal in 1980
and the Order of Canada in 1992.

Though Carrier has written movingly of the cruelty of urban isola-
tion, his most celebrated novels are set in deceptively simple, almost
mythical villages in the Quebec countryside with evocative names

such as Saint-Toussaint-des-Saints.

Carrier's own life began in such a place: the Beauce village of Sainte-Justine-de-Dorchester where he was born one of six children. His mother was a teacher, his father a travelling salesman who had left school very young. Reared in an oral tradition where storytelling was a natural form of entertainment, Carrier was sent away to boarding school at age eleven. His father, a fan of Duplessis, entertained the fond ambition that Roch would become prime minister of Canada and protect the rights of French Canadians. The son eventually decided that literature made a more powerful use of his talents than did politics.

Educated at Collège Saint-Louis in Edmunston, New Brunswick, at the Université de Montréal and at the Sorbonne from where he holds a doctorate in French literature, Carrier returned to Montreal in 1964 to the energizing effects of the Quiet Revolution. His early work was stamped with brash nationalist and anti-clerical sentiments. "I expressed in my first books my frustration, my despair, my anger, my hope as a young French Canadian. I was labelled a separatist. But I was not one. I never believed that Quebec had to jump out of Canada to solve its problems," he wrote in *Canadian Living* magazine.

Carrier's first novel, *La Guerre, Yes Sir!*, launched a trilogy that has become a Canadian classic. He wrote it in a white heat, in twelve days ("But I had done a lot of preliminary writing before," he told me recently in an interview at his Westmount home. "It's like when one prepares whipping cream, if you like. One beats for a long time, and then all of a sudden the cream appears.") Couched in the tone of a folktale and set in a small village in Quebec, *La Guerre* begins with a shocking scene in which a young man cuts off his hand to avoid the draft. Dramatic in form and content, the novel takes place in one day and revolves around the corpse of Corriveau, a young villager killed in World War II who is brought home by an honour guard of English-Canadian soldiers, ubiquitously referred to as *maudits Anglais*.

La Guerre received an enthusiastic response. "(This) is a first novel of staggering sophistication and control, proving that there exists in Montreal a major international writer," wrote a critic in the *Journal of Commonwealth Literature*. Almost twenty years and eight novels later, Mark Abley in *Saturday Night* compared Carrier's 1984 novel

De l'Amour dans la Ferraille (translated in 1987 as *Heartbreaks Along the Road*) to Salman Rushdie's *Midnight's Children* and Gabriel Garcia Marquez's *One Hundred Years of Solitude* for its power to "transform and illuminate a fragment of the visible world with the grace and force of myth."

Not all the critics agreed. In taking his inspiration from the rural past, Carrier bucks contemporary trends in Québécois literature. His use of folk stereotypes has sometimes been viewed as pandering to outdated English-Canadian perceptions of the province. His political views—which have evolved into an unabashed Canadian patriotism—have also been decidedly unfashionable in Quebec, at the same time as they have won him friends in the rest of Canada.

Carrier, who had written *La Guerre, Yes Sir!* with such passionate speed, took more than three years to create *Heartbreaks Along the Road*, an extended modern fable about political corruption in the time of Duplessis, his most ambitious book to date. The mixed critical response to it led to a hiatus of several years in a prolific writing career.

But he has bounced back with a spate of new books in the last couple of years. He works instinctively, writing only when he feels inspired. "Writing is a magic act," he has said to Marie-Claire Girard of *Le Devoir*, "maybe even replacing prayer." Humour, too, has a spiritual quality for him. "Humour is an exercise of the soul."

In mining the terrain that he knows so well, Carrier continues to break new ground, experimenting with form and content. "I know," he told me, "that many artists try to find in the world some kind of coherence and to translate that kind of coherence into coherent works.... (But) for me, life is a bloody beautiful mess (*un sacré beau désordre*). That's what's absolutely fascinating about it. I don't try to see order in it. What interests me is the beautiful mess, which men and women try to disentangle. That's what's exciting! And that's what I write about."

Excerpt from *La Guerre, Yes Sir!*, translated by Sheila Fischman (Toronto: Anansi, 1970), 5-6.

Joseph wasn't panting.
He approached like a man walking to work. Which hand

would he put on the log, his right hand or his left? His right hand was stronger, better for working. His left hand was strong too. Joseph spread the five fingers of his left hand on the log.

He heard breathing behind him. He turned around. It was his own.

His other fingers, his other hand, seized the axe. It crashed down between the wrist and the hand, which leapt into the snow and was slowly drowned by his blood.

Joseph did not see the red stain or the hand or the snow. When the axe cut through the bone Joseph felt only a warm caress; his suffering began when it was buried in the wood. The cloudy window separating him from life gradually became very clear, transparent. In a moment of dizzy lucidity Joseph was aware of the fear that had tortured him for months:

Their Christly shells would have made jam out of me..." He drove his stump into the snow. "They've already made jam out of Corriveau with their goddam war... They won't get me... me, I'll be making jam next fall: strawberries, blueberries, gooseberries, red apples, raspberries..."

Joseph burst into a great laugh, which he could hear going up very high, up above the snow. He hadn't had so much fun since the beginning of the war. The villagers heard his voice. He was calling for help.

SELECTED BIBLIOGRAPHY

La Guerre, Yes Sir! (Montreal: Éditions du Jour, 1968); translated by Sheila Fischman, (Toronto, Anansi, 1970).

Floralie, Où Es-tu? (Montreal: Éditions du Jour, 1969); translated by Sheila Fischman as *Floralie, Where Are You?*, (Toronto, Anansi, 1971).

La Dame Qui Avait des Chaînes aux Chevilles (Montreal: Stanké, 1981); translated by Sheila Fischman as *Lady with Chains*, (Toronto, Anansi, 1984).

De l'Amour dans la Ferraille (Montreal: Stanké, 1984); translated by Sheila Fischman as *Heartbreaks Along the Road*, (Toronto, Anansi, 1987).

L'Ange de la Solitude (Montreal: VLB, 1989).

MARIE-CLAIRE BLAIS

Restless Experimenter

THE PUBLICATION OF MARIE-CLAIRE BLAIS' *La Belle bête* in 1959 caused a literary sensation in a Quebec on the eve of the Quiet Revolution. Readers were either mesmerized or repelled by the book's subject matter and style. It went through two editions in six weeks, within a year it was translated into English as *Mad Shadows*.

The story focuses on the erotic love of a mother for her beautiful mindless son and the hatred felt for him by his envious ugly sister. The elemental emotions revealed culminate in a horrific climax of murder, betrayal and disfigurement.

The author of this surreal and nightmarish fable—written in a white heat of fifteen days—was a slight, convent-bred girl of nineteen who shrank from all hint of publicity. Since the age of eleven she had displayed a single-minded and tenacious desire to become a writer, though almost everything in her background militated against it.

Born in 1939 to a mother who had been a teacher and to a factory-worker father, Marie-Claire Blais grew up in the working class district of Limoilou in Quebec City, the oldest of five children.

She won a scholarship to a convent school "but," she adds with a quick laugh in a recent, rare interview, "I was never a very good student." She was a voracious reader though, and the works of Malraux and Camus influenced her greatly in her early teens. At sixteen, coming across the novels of the Brontë sisters, she wrote copy-cat versions of her own.

By this time she had had to quit school and was working at a succession of drone-like jobs—in a cookie factory, as a bank cashier and

155

a salesgirl ("all with an absence of enthusiasm that exasperated my employers," she has written). Her parents, even though they considered her obsession with writing a "futile misery," fixed up a little worktable for her in their bedroom where she could write.

"Writing," she told me, "was always like an angel over my head. It gave me faith."

Though she is strongly anti-clerical, she gratefully acknowledges that her first mentor was a priest. Père Georges-Henri Lévesque of Laval University introduced her to her first publisher.

The setting for her second great break was the "the slightly faded charm" of the Café de Paris in Montreal's Ritz-Carlton Hotel. At twenty-two, the author of a second novel, *Tête Blanche*, and in love with a Montreal filmmaker, Blais moved to Montreal and set herself up in a rooming house on Prince Arthur Street. A year in Paris followed on a Canada Council grant. "But the thing that really changed my life ... was praise and understanding from the great (American) critic, Edmund Wilson" whom she met in 1962 at the Ritz.

In *O Canada: An American's Notes on Canadian Culture* (1965), the book of criticism which largely put Quebec on the literary map in the English-speaking world, Wilson pronounced Marie-Claire Blais "a true phenomenon; she may possibly be a genius. At the age of twenty-four, she has produced four remarkable books of a passionate and poetic force that, as far as my reading goes, is not otherwise to be found in French Canadian fiction." This glowing endorsement was all the more meaningful in that Wilson had a decided bias against women writers.

He sponsored her for two Guggenheim grants, freeing her to write full time. Blais moved for several years to Massachusetts. Here she entered into a lengthy love and work relationship with the Philadelphia-born painter, Mary Meigs, charted movingly by the latter in two works of autobiography, *Lily Briscoe: A Self-Portrait* and *The Medusa Head*. (Meigs also illustrated a deluxe edition of Blais' *A Season in the Life of Emmanuel*. No longer lovers, they remain steadfast friends.)

Blais' dizzying prolificity continued. She has gone on to write more than thirty books—mainly novels and novellas—and several plays and collections of poetry. She has won the Prix France-Québec and the prestigious French Prix Médicis for *A Season in the Life of Emmanuel* which was translated into thirteen languages (including Japanese, Hungarian and Czech); the Governor General's Award twice (for *The Manuscripts of Pauline Archange* in 1968, and *Deaf to the City* in 1979); the Prix David for the totality of her work; and has been named to the Order of Canada. In May 1993, she was made a member of Belgium's Royal Academy of French Language and Literature, the first non-European to receive the honour.

A perfectionistic and meticulous researcher, Blais is a restless ex-perimenter with language and form, her work imbued with a dark vision of evil at the heart of things. (She herself strenuously resists being labelled sombre and in person bubbles with laughter and shy charm.) Quebec critics have in particular castigated her for bleakness of vision, yet she has been known to write satire (*St. Lawrence Blues* satirizes working-class Montreal) and even *A Season in the Life of Emmanuel* contains some bitingly humorous passages.

This novel and *The Manuscripts of Pauline Archange*, both dealing with the subject of tormented children in poverty-stricken families, are among her most highly-praised. Alienation, solitude, marginality and revolt have continued to be her major themes. Her later works, while retaining mythic and surrealistic overtones, have tended to become more realistic. Some are set in the gay bars of Montreal and Paris. In others, such as *Anna's World* and the recently translated *Pierre*, she pleads for a peaceful, healthy world through an apocalyptic view of contemporary life.

Describing herself as a vagabond spirit and still intensely private, Blais travels a great deal. "I need to be in perpetual motion, travel-ling, writing as I go, wherever my needs or my phantasy tells me to go," she has written. She spends considerable time in Key West, Florida, but maintains a pied-à-terre in Montreal and a residence in the Eastern Townships, her preferred writing place.

She has resisted political engagement and nationalist labels. "I am an engaged writer in the sense of humanism," she told Nicole Aas-Rouxparis in *The Journal of Canadian Studies*. "That's all. What tortures me is the fragility of people, how easily they crumble."

Excerpt from *The Manuscripts of Pauline Archange*, translated by Derek Coltman (New York: Bantam Books, 1976), 34-35.

Along the whole length of our path through childhood, until we reached those lucid shadows that mark its end, two powers held continual sway: the first disciplinary and destructive, that of the whip; and the other resulting from it, in a remorse-soaked sweetness, the power of pursuit, of seduction, of the rape of bodies—and souls perhaps—against which judgment is powerless, for which it can have only pity. Wounds inflicted, wounds closing up alone in silence, or too deep to heal at all, or too shameful to be admitted, all the laws of terror cloaked each individual being so utterly as to make him invisible to his fellow creatures. By living too much in the company of misted mirrors that lie as they reflect you, you can become a stranger to your own image. My mother, who because of her illness used to be visited once a week by a young Franciscan to whom she made her scrupulous confessions, was involuntarily to close her eyes later on, when I was almost twelve, to the unfortunate frailties this priest exhibited when alone with me—against my will, but a will there was no one to defend. "What's all that blood on your legs? You've gone and scratched yourself again, climbing like a boy as usual, I suppose. When will you start to be sensible like other people?" my mother scolded, in that simplicity of hers that would never have ventured to formulate even the idea of such evil, let alone dare to attack "religion in person," of which the mystical Franciscan with his wandering eyes, of whose strange behavior once outside her room, she remained wholly unaware, was a representative. If I wept or moaned while in his grip, my mother, as she lay vomiting on the other side of the wall, was in too much pain herself to hear me. Nor did this interplay of sufferings include any corresponding consolation in its pattern: my mother always tried to clean up all traces of her sickness behind her, so as not to drive my father to despair, and I on my side used to bury my bloodied clothing deep in earth. Was this long silence to become one day the redemption of mankind? So my mother believed, as her eyes avoided mine during the daily recitation of my catechism lesson beside her bed: "Purity, hope, charity..."

SELECTED BIBLIOGRAPHY

La Belle bête (Quebec: Institut Littéraire du Québec, 1959); translated by Merloyd Lawrence as *Mad Shadows* (Toronto: McClelland & Stewart, 1960).

Tête Blanche (Quebec: Institut Littéraire du Québec, 1960); translated by Charles Fullman (Toronto: McClelland & Stewart, 1961).

Une Saison dans la vie d'Émmanuel (Montreal: Éditions du Jour, 1965); translated by Derek Coltman as *A Season in the Life of Emmanuel* (New York: Farrar, Straus & Giroux, 1966).

Les Manuscrits de Pauline Archange (Montreal: Éditions du Jour, 1968); translated by Derek Coltman with *Vivre! Vivre!* (1969) as *The Manuscripts of Pauline Archange* (Toronto: McClelland & Stewart, 1982).

Le Sourd dans la ville (Montreal: Stanké, 1979); translated by Carol Dunlop as *Deaf to the City* (Toronto: Lester & Orpen Dennys, 1980).

L'Ange de la solitude (Montreal: VLB, 1989).

JOVETTE MARCHESSAULT
A Magnificent Voyage

WHEN ADULTS USED TO ASK HER what she wanted to be when she grew up, the child Jovette Marchessault would answer, "I want to write." On Friday evenings her grandmother would bring her books which the little girl read deep into the night: books by the Brontë sisters, by Jules Verne, Charles Dickens, Rudyard Kipling.

Jovette Marchessault would indeed become a prize-winning novelist and playwright—after she had worked as a visual artist and exhibited her masks, sculptures, drawings and frescoes at galleries in Montreal, Toronto, New York, Paris and Brussels. But, despite her early commitment, Marchessault's road to fiery creativity was blocked for decades.

She grew up in poverty, outraged and in rebellion against the cycle of family violence she witnessed in her Plateau Mont Royal neighbourhood. She quit school at age thirteen to work. Her first job was at a diaper service—("You could have cut that smell with a knife into thick slices," she has written in *La Mère des herbes* (*Mother of the Grass*, the second volume of her autobiographical trilogy)—followed by a sweatshop in Montreal's garment industry. Then, for nearly twenty years, she had a series of clerical jobs, rising to the position of assistant credit manager at the Grolier encyclopaedia company.

In 1969 she came to a crossroads. She realized she must either create or suffocate.

Marchessault was born in 1938 into a working class family of mixed Cree Indian and French-Canadian origins. The two great positive

161

influences of her childhood were periods spent in the semi-rural ambience of the Bout de l'Isle section of Pointe-aux-Trembles in Montreal's easternmost corner, and her close relationship with her grandmother, an extraordinary woman. The first rooted her in a love and first-hand knowledge of nature. The second gave her a mentor with unusual strength of character, inspiring creativity and experience of native lore that would one day feed Marchessault's art and writing.

It was only when her grandmother died in 1969 that Marchessault quit the jobs that hemmed her in and moved to a cabin in the woods to write. Defeated by the tyranny of the blank page, in desperation she turned to painting.

I interviewed Marchessault in the sun-filled Westmount living room of artist and author Mary Meigs whom she was visiting for the day from the Eastern Townships farm where she now lives year-round. In an unexpected turn of the conversation, Marchessault spoke with earnest eloquence of her gratitude to members of Montreal's Jewish community whose initial support for her art enabled her to establish herself.

Future gallery-owner Lois Shane, then a graduate student in English literature, fell in love with Marchessault's paintings at a time when the artist was a total unknown. Shane offered to exhibit Marchessault's work in her home. "I didn't speak any English and she didn't speak any French, but there was instant sympathy between us. And she hung my paintings in her house and stacked them on the floors and invited all her friends... Every one of them was sold."

Marchessault supported herself by her art for five years. And when she finally took another stab at writing in 1974, her writer's block had dissolved.

Comme une enfant de la terre (*Like a Child of the Earth*) won the France-Quebec Prize in 1976. A highly original, lyrical and often polemical novel, it begins and ends with the narrator's birth. As in the sequel, *Mother of the Grass*, Marchessault stretches the boundaries of autobiography to include mythic and visionary experiences. In both these poetic and heartfelt books, she is interested in reclaiming her native heritage, subtly linking the oppression of Amerindians with the historical stifling of women's creativity.

At that time a radical lesbian feminist, Marchessault's writing throbbed with anger at the cycle of violence she witnessed in many of her friends' families as a child. "All the fathers had erections in the course of the whirlwind-cyclone, their little girls' floods of tears, their reddened skin, their humiliation, their agony; they took the time to have an erection. They had hard-ons in their heads and came while beating their children."

In the late 1970s, Marchessault began to write for the stage. Her plays make highly original use of details from the lives of women writers and artists to reinterpret, from a feminist perspective, both religion and history. Steeped in rich imagery and taking enormous liberties with the biographical facts, *La Saga des poules mouillées (Saga of the Wet Hens)*, for instance, stages a mythical encounter between four Quebec women writers: Laure Conan, Germaine Guèvremont, Gabrielle Roy and Anne Hébert. Other plays treat the lives of Anaïs Nin, Violette Leduc and Gertrude Stein.

Marchessault has won the Governor General's Award for drama for her 1990 play, *The Magnificent Voyage of Emily Carr*. Her works have been performed in New York, Sherbrooke, Toronto, Vancouver, Victoria, as well as in Montreal.

Infused with a vision of the universe in which everything is interconnected, in recent years her world view has become more inclusive, more tending towards a reconciliation between the sexes, between parents and children, humans and animals. A cycle of three plays which began with *Demande de travail sur les lumineuses* (1988)— a utopian piece set on the eve of the twenty-first century exploring relationships in a nuclear family—looks toward the day, "When we will know everything. All will be said. All tears will be dried, all the bowed backs will straighten."

Imagining something totally new is key to her work. "I don't work in naturalistic theatre, my plays don't take place in the kitchen as you wash the dishes, or in the bedroom. I can be by the seashore and in the stars and anywhere! So I can take all sorts of liberties and take all sorts of pleasure in imagining things."

Excerpt from *La Mère des herbes*, translated by Yvonne Klein as *Mother of the Grass* (Vancouver: Talonbooks, 1989), 39-40. The children have been stealing apples from Old man Pépin's orchard and he has retaliated by setting traps.

The next morning well before daybreak, I heard my grandmother open the door to the backyard. There were a few metallic noises and then silence. I saw her reappear a few minutes later. She crossed the clover field which led to the orchard, bearing some tools in her hands. What were they? I did not know. It was still dark out and she seemed to me very much alone and very fragile in the clover field.

"Little one," she often used to say to me, "you have to be full of strength. You have to have as much strength as you have blood in your body. Someday you'll see that there is as much blood in a woman's body as there is water in a lake."

I stayed by the window all the time she was gone. From here, if I let go of my body and all my emotions, I could catch a glimpse of the promised land. The sort of day it would be was getting itself ready in the air, gently simmering, drop by drop, building itself brick by brick. Oh, if only you could build happiness the same way. Little by little, the sky allowed itself to be overwhelmed by the trails of red and pink and yellow in the great silence.

Grandmother came back when the sky was yellow, the last stage before the blue of this lovely day upon the earth. She crossed the field with her seven-league boots, a strained look on her face. Her two arms, her two hands, her ten fingers bore four traps, four engines ready to snap your tender skin with all the ferocity of a human jaw. Under her arms were the tools which she had used to spring the traps and to free the rough trunk of the apple tree from its black chains. … Then I heard her come in and open the doors, open tins, shake down the stove, strike a match, beat the eggs, and answer her husband's questions.

"It's done. The traps are wrapped in paper in the garbage can."

"You didn't see anybody?"

"I did the right thing."

Comme une enfant de la terre (Montreal: Leméac, 1975), translated by Yvonne Klein as *Like a Child of the Earth* (Vancouver: Talonbooks, 1988).

La Mère des herbes (Montreal: Quinze, 1980), translated as *Mother of the Grass* by Yvonne Klein (Vancouver: Talonbooks, 1989).

La Saga des poules mouillées (Montreal: Théâtre du Nouveau Monde, 1981), translated by Linda Gaboriau as *Saga of the Wet Hens* (Vancouver: Talonbooks, 1983).

The Magnificent Voyage of Emily Carr translated from the French play *Le Voyage magnifique d'Emily Carr* by Linda Gaboriau (Vancouver: Talonbooks, 1992).

L'AVALÉE
DES AVALÉS

roman

par

RÉJEAN DUCHARME

RÉJEAN DUCHARME

The Great (D)evader

"MY WORK IS PUBLIC, BUT NOT ME. I don't want my face known, I don't want any connection made between me and my novel."

The photographs that represent Réjean Ducharme are of a very young man; recent ones are unavailable. Interviewed in 1966 by the poet (and future Parti Québécois Cabinet minister) Gérald Godin, at twenty-five Ducharme staked out the position of obsessive privacy that he has maintained for more than a quarter of a century. One of Quebec's most original authors, he is, without question, its most mysterious and reclusive.

In 1965, Ducharme had submitted the manuscript of his novel *L'Avalée des avalés* (*The Swallower Swallowed*) to a Montreal publishing house, only to have it promptly returned. Not skipping a beat, he despatched the manuscript—along with two other earlier novels— to France's most distinguished publisher, Éditions Gallimard. Gallimard published all three: *L'Avalée des avalés* in 1966, *Le Nez qui voque* in 1967 and *L'Océantume* in 1968.

The publication of *L'Avalée des avalés* was a literary event: it was immediately translated into four languages and its author hailed a genius. Hounded by journalists, Ducharme changed residence almost day by day. Rumours and accusations flew that a youthful Quebecer could not have produced such a work of genius. Jean-Paul Sartre and Naïm Kattan were some of the names bandied about as the possible authors of the book. (In 1991, a year after the publication of *Dévadé*, Ducharme's first novel in fourteen years, his identity was once more a news item: based on an anonymous source, an article in

167

La Presse hypothesized that the true author of his books was the late actress Luce Guilbeault.)

Biographical details of Ducharme's life are, of necessity, sketchy. He was born in the small town of Saint-Félix-de-Valois in 1941, the son of Nina and Omer Ducharme. In a brief 1968 interview with Hermine Beauregard in *Châtelaine*, Ducharme confided that, in the midst of a large family, he had spent a solitary childhood. He attended classical college in Joliette and, for a semester, Montreal's École Polytechnique. A grab bag of occupations followed: encyclopaedia salesman, theatre usher, proofreader. For a short period, he even trained in the Royal Canadian Air Force.

Given this incomplete author profile and the astonishing virtuosity of *L'Avalée des avalés*, for a time Ducharme aroused insatiable curiosity among both the Quebec and French public. Nominated for France's prestigious Prix Goncourt, his book won the Governor General's Award for fiction in 1967. Ducharme has also received another Governor General's prize for his play *HA ha!* (he has written four plays altogether); the Prix littéraire de la Province de Québec for the novel *Le Nez qui voque*; the Belgium-Canada Prize for *L'Hiver du force* (1973, subsequently translated as *Wild to Mild*); the France-Canada Prize for *Les Enfantômes* in 1976; and, most recently in 1990, the $100,000 inaugural Prix Gilles Corbeil awarded by the Émile Nelligan Foundation for achievements in French-language literature by a North American.

His works include seven novels (Charles Foran in *Saturday Night* called the most recent, *Dévadé*, "perhaps the most textured"); screenplays for the films *Les Bons débarras* and *Les Beaux souvenirs*; lyrics for a number of Robert Charlebois' songs; and three visual art collections under the name of Roch Plante.

Many of Ducharme's novels feature children or adolescents in revolt against the hypocrisy of adult society. In *L'Avalée des avalés*, the heroine, Bernice Einberg, daughter of a Catholic mother and a Jewish father, expresses her hatred of everything she can't fully possess by inventing her own language, an incomprehensible, anti-social tongue called "Bernician".

Pain underlies Bernice's plight, as it does those of the rada, Ducharme's term for the misfits and dropouts who people *Dévadé*.

What redeems the pervasive pessimism of his vision (in *Dévadé*, life is compared to a garbage can) is the dense, often lyrical prose and a brilliant shattering of the normal conventions of language. Critic Patricia Smart has called his style a kind of "literary terrorism, building elaborate word-plays that simultaneously provoke interpretation and confound meaning."

Only two of Ducharme's novels and one play have been translated into English, his linguistic richness and playfulness stumping most attempts at crossing the language divide. But even in the original French, Ducharme is no easy ride. The distinguished critic Gilles Marcotte once called his works "both the apotheosis and the negation of the novel."

Excerpt from *L'Avalée des avalés*, translated by Barbara Bray as *The Swallower Swallowed* (London: Hamish Hamilton, 1968), 6.

I am alone. I have only to shut my eyes to see it. If you want to know where you are you shut your eyes. You're where you are when you shut your eyes; in the dark, in the void. There is my mother and father and my brother Christian, and Constance Chlore. But they're not where I am when I shut my eyes. There's no one, never anyone but me. No need to bother about other people: they're somewhere else. When I talk or play with other people I feel quite clearly that they're outside, that they can't enter where I am and I can't enter where they are. I know that, as soon as their voices stop preventing me from hearing my silence, loneliness and fear will take hold of me again. No point in bothering about what happens on the surface of the earth or of the water. It doesn't affect what goes on in the dark and the void. Just waiting all the time. Wanting for you to do something to make it pass, so as to escape. Other people are far away. They fly away like butterflies. A butterfly is as far away as the firmament, even when you're holding it in your hand. No point in bothering about butterflies; that's only suffering for nothing. There's nothing here but me.

L'Avalée des avalés, (Paris: Gallimard, 1966); translated by Barbara Bray as *The Swallower Swallowed* (London: Hamish Hamilton, 1968). *L'Hiver de force* (Paris: Gallimard, 1973); translated by Robert Guy Scully as *Wild to Mild* (Saint-Lambert, Quebec: Héritage, 1980). *Dévadé* (Paris: Gallimard/Lacomb, 1990).

YVES BEAUCHEMIN

Writing for Pleasure

THOUGH WRITING DOESN'T COME EASILY to Yves Beauchemin—his hefty novels take years to craft and go through many rewrites—his work is fueled by the pleasure principle. "I want to give pleasure to the reader," Beauchemin has said on many occasions. "Literature is about plea-sure."

His readers would agree. Beauchemin's two blockbuster novels, *Le Matou* (*The Alleycat*) and *Juliette Pomerleau* (*Juliette* in English trans-lation), were the best- and third best-selling Quebec books of the 1980s respectively (Arlette Cousture's two-volume *Les Filles du Caleb* came second). *Le Matou* has sold well over one million copies in fifteen languages—including Swedish, Spanish and Hebrew. Beauchemin's enormous popularity in France (where *Le Matou* sold 750,000 copies) has, to a large extent, enabled him to write full-time since 1983. Many of the literary prizes he has won have had a strong popular base: for instance, both *Le Matou* and *Juliette Pomerleau* have taken the People's Choice prizes at Montreal's Salon du Livre.

Beauchemin was also the recipient of the Prix France-Québec for his first published novel *L'Enfirouapé* (which dealt with the October Crisis of 1970); the Prix des Jeunes Romanciers du Journal de Montréal; and the Prix de la Communauté Urbaine de Montréal. In France, Beauchemin has won the Prix Jean Giono, the *Elle* magazine readers' prize and the Prix du Roman de l'Été.

Yves Beauchemin was born in Noranda in 1941 but moved with his family to the northern-Quebec logging community of Clova in

Abitibi when he was five. In *Du Sommet d'un arbre*, a collection of autobiographical radio essays, Beauchemin recalled his childhood as one of total freedom, with the run of both the countryside and the industrial buildings of the Canadian International Company for whom his father worked as a forestry expert.

He was a voracious reader from early childhood, "infected" by his mother with "the reading virus," he has written. Born nearly blind in his left eye, he couldn't do team sports, but excelled in all games that required imaginative inventiveness. (In a recent interview, he laughingly told me, "It's because of my eye that I became a writer.") Some critics have found seeds of the raciness and episodic quality of his novels in his early love of American comics such as Archie and Batman. More commonly, however, his sprawling and densely-written works are compared to the nineteenth-century greats: Dickens, Zola, Balzac, even Dostoyevski.

Beauchemin began to write in his teens while attending classical college in Joliette; by the time he was twenty-five he had written about forty short stories. His arrival to Montreal in 1962 to attend university had a profound effect on him. "A great city is an inexhaustible subject," he told Stephen Godfrey of the *Globe & Mail* on 1990, and Montreal and its suburbs spring to vivid life in his novels.

Montreal was also the crucible of his political awakening. Confronted in the early 1960s by unilingual English signs and a French-language majority, Beauchemin became a committed and hardline *indépendantiste*. (His brilliant analogy of Quebec as a cube of sugar next to a gallon of coffee has been widely quoted.)

Beauchemin's immense popularity can be traced to his dynamic and upbeat literary outlook. His work diverges sharply from the deep strain of pessimism and malaise that characterizes much of French-Canadian writing. Florent Boissonneault's struggles in *Le Matou* to establish himself as a successful entrepreneur may be epic and uphill, but at the conclusion of the story he remains essentially what he was at its outset, "a young man ... with a twinkle in his eye."

Beauchemin's books are plot driven and peopled by engaging and highly original characters defined through their actions and not their psyches, and often drawn from life. In *Juliette*, the big-hearted (and vastly-proportioned) title character was inspired by an immense and likable cleaning woman at Radio-Québec where Beauchemin worked from 1969 to 1983; her introverted great-nephew was patterned on one of Beauchemin's own sons; the composer Bohuslav Martinek was born out of Beauchemin's affinity for the Czech composer Bohuslav Martinu.

Beauchemin has also published two works for children and written the libretto for Jacques Hétu's opera, *Le Prix*, (*The Prize*).

His Balzacian verve has been both praised and criticized. While his plots and characters are marvellously inventive, their want of psychological depth is at times disconcerting. And while one of the most appealing aspects of Beauchemin's world is the lack of overt politicizing (Quebec is presented without fuss as an apparently autonomous political entity), anglophone readers have accused him of xenophobia for his creation of the mysterious Egon Ratablavasky character in *Le Matou*. A devil incarnate who plots the downfall of the engaging protagonists for no apparent reason, Ratablavasky exudes a dreadful smell and speaks with a peculiar accent.

The accusation of xenophobia has stung Beauchemin and made him leery of the anglophone press. He was skittish about setting up an interview with me, telling me over the phone, "I am like Mordecai Richler, people attribute things to us that we haven't said or done."

But, when we finally met at the Bistro St. Denis, he was charm personified, courteously searching for the English translation of a French word when the sense of something eluded me. He insisted, however, that we steer clear of politics because, "Convincing an English-Canadian of the necessity of Quebec independence—it's a long time since I abandoned that idea! It's like taking this restaurant here, lifting it up in one's hand and moving it to Mont Saint-Bruno. *That* would be easier... Our interests are so divergent that it's wasting time."

In any case, he doesn't believe in mixing politics and literature, and he pointedly emphasized that, in contemporary literature, his favourite writers are the Americans. "Literature in France, as far as I can see, ... smells of an office. Whereas American literature, it smells of gin, it smells of the street, it smells of garbage,... it smells of life."

Posterity will decide whether or not Quebec's literary superstar is a great writer. In the meantime, though, millions of readers will

happily attest that he makes a great read.
Excerpt from *Le Matou*, translated by Sheila Fischman as *The Alleycat*
(Toronto: McClelland & Stewart, 1986), 135.

At ten o'clock on the morning of November 30, 1974, the
bells of St-Pierre-Claver church on St-Joseph Boulevard start to
ring as usual, but more than one passerby turns around, puzzled
by their tone, which is somehow different. The notes sound dry
and choked, and they drop like balls of lead, leaving no echo.
Confused and vaguely unpleasant memories are aroused. People
try for a moment to identify them, until the flow of daily thoughts
resumes its course.

The sky today is one of solid cloud. It bulges weightily over
the city and you would look in vain for the sun, which it seems
to have swallowed. Some light sifts down from it, gray and pow-
dery. It hardens the outlines of every object and comes crashing
down on surfaces. The air stings your eyes, numbs fingertips
and forces legs to move quickly. The mood is one of anxious
waiting. Strangers on the sidewalk catch themselves staring at
one another, not knowing what to say. And suddenly a minus-
cule event occurs. A snowflake appears from the void, swirls
through the air and begins a cautious descent broken by pauses,
as if it were afraid of shattering its complex, fragile form, before
coming to rest on the ground and disappearing.

Winter has arrived. Metal doorknobs turn to ice. More
snowflakes appear, discrete, almost foolish amid so much space,
but their number keeps growing, and soon the colour of the
streets has softened.

SELECTED BIBLIOGRAPHY
L'Enfirouapé (Montreal: La Presse, 1974).
Le Matou (Montreal: Editions Québec/Amérique, 1981); translated
by Sheila Fischman as *The Alleycat* (Toronto: McClelland & Stewart,
1986).
Du Sommet d'un arbre (Montreal: Editions Québec/Amérique, 1986).
Juliette Pomerleau (Montreal: Éditions Québec/Amérique, 1989)
translated by Sheila Fischman as *Juliette* (Toronto: McClelland &
Stewart, 1993).

MICHEL TREMBLAY

Bard of Plateau Mont Royal

MICHEL TREMBLAY WAS BORN, the youngest of five children, in 1942, to an elderly couple in a yellow brick house on rue Fabre in the heart of Plateau Mont Royal. He was a planned child, he has written in his recent autobiographical work *Douze coups de théâtre*, born of his parents' grief at the loss of two other children who died at the beginning of the war. ("I arrived in their life like a gift from heaven, a treasure that they prized more than any other in the world.") Poverty squeezed three families—twelve people—into seven rooms. Until he was six, he ate in a high chair; until he was nine, he slept in a crib. He was brought up by six women.

"My first vision of the world was of these women who forgot that I was there and who said things they would never have said had they known I was listening," he told *L'Actualité* in May 1992.

Elsewhere, alluding to the impact of privation and intellectual aridity on his extended family, he has said, "one or two people came out of it. Others were handicapped for life and today some of them haunt prisons and asylums."

Michel Tremblay has mined both the emotional and physical terrain of his formative years in twenty-one plays and an extended cycle of novels, frequently using the same semi-autobiographical characters in both his drama and fiction. He has raised this cast to the level of universality and high art, even as they speak a *joual* whose cultural significance and linguisitic validity have been a moot point in Quebec. (The Quebec government refused to pay travel expenses for the 1972 Paris engagement of *Les Belles-soeurs* because of its use of *joual*; among Tremblay's many honours is that of Chevalier de l'Ordre des Arts et des Lettres of France "pour avoir bien utilisé la langue française.")

As an avowed separatist, he refused to allow the performance of his plays in English in Montreal until after the Parti Québécois electoral win in 1976. They are now presented regularly at Stratford and across the country.

In fact, Tremblay is the first Canadian playwright to achieve international renown. Critics have compared him to Molière and to Gabriel Garcia Marquez. His plays have been translated into, among other languages, Spanish, Polish, Yiddish and Scots, and have been staged from Anchorage to Tokyo. *Les Belles-soeurs* has outsold every other contemporary French play in the world.

In addition to his prolific output of plays and novels, Tremblay has also translated and adapted drama from other languages into French, written screenplays, musicals, the libretto for the opera *Nelligan*, and has embarked on a series of memoirs using his associations to the films and plays of his childhood and youth as the springboard for autobiography.

As a young child, Tremblay spent his holidays inventing new endings for familiar fairy tales; one of his imaginary childhood creations was a giant whose heart was lodged in his big toe. As an adolescent, he attended the theatre regularly and—forbidden by his parents— secretly. He has written in *Douze coups de théâtre*, "For me, probably because it was forbidden, the theatre was a place that was sealed and a bit suspect, where one could reveal secret things you could never say on television."

Though he wanted to be a writer, because of an innate defeatism inherited from his parents who thought he would starve if he pursued his ambitions, he had little faith in his ability to become one. When he won a scholarship to a classical college, disaffected by its snobbery, he only lasted a few months. "I remember the morning I left," he told me in a recent interview, laughing at the naiveté and pretentiousness of youth, "I slammed the door after saying to the class—I was fourteen—'One day you will hear from me!'"

Thirsting for knowledge, he read his way through the classical curriculum on his own. That classical influence would, in fact, mark his future plays both in terms of structure and his frequent use of a Greek chorus.

When he left school, Tremblay followed the family trade of linotypist—and saw every movie and piece of theatre in town. (This habit has not left him. These days, he writes in the mornings, then goes to the movies or the theatre.) Winning the Radio-Canada young authors competition in 1964—for a play that he had written five years earlier but had not had the courage to submit—marked an important turning point in his career. So did his teaming up with André Brassard which dates from the same period. Brassard's brilliant interpretation of Tremblay's plays for the stage contributed significantly to their initial success.

Tremblay wrote *Les Belles-soeurs* in three weeks in 1965; it premiered at the Théâtre du Rideau Vert in 1968. On the surface, a naturalistic slice-of-life about a woman who wins a million trading stamps and invites her relatives and friends to a stamp-pasting party, the play explores themes of "la maudite vie plate": the senseless daily routine and cultural impotence of the working class in east end Montreal. With its bold use of soliloquies and choruses, its streaks of burlesque and its *joual* idiom, it was immediately hailed as a breakthrough—and roundly condemned as vulgar.

As openly homosexual from adolescence as one could be in the 1950s ("I never had a girlfriend, but I never talked about such things with my parents," he said to me), Tremblay has resisted the label of gay writer.

For instance, his 1986 novel *Le Coeur découvert*—translated as *The Heart Laid Bare* by Sheila Fischman—and its recently-released sequel, *Le Coeur éclaté*, poignantly present homosexual love as a slight mutation on the garden-variety type and unabashedly aim at winning understanding from a general audience. "When I talk about (homosexuality), I talk about it in a way that is not addressed to gay people only. So that everybody can read my novels and plays and identify even with the gay characters. I work on that very, very hard."

Despite all his success (recent awards include four honorary degrees, one of them from Stirling University in Scotland), Tremblay remains astonishingly vulnerable to even the possibility of critical or popular disapprobation. On the eve of publication of *Le Coeur éclaté*, he confided, "It will be horrible for me, if for one reason or another, (critics or public) get away from me for a book or for a play... You write because you want to be told you're good."

In the past, he has been attacked for an unrelenting pessimism, what some critics have called his *misérabilisme*. In fact, in its totality, Tremblay's work offers a harrowing view of both the Québécois proletarian family and of the marginalized and promiscuous denizens of the Main, Boulevard Saint Laurent: prostitutes, transvestites, cheap entertainers.

But in its epic ability to probe psychic pain and—as Robert Lévesque has written in *Le Devoir*—to "find the colour of emotions, the scent of memories," Tremblay's writing soars to a redemptive love.

Excerpt from *La Grosse femme d'à côté est enceinte*, translated by Sheila Fischman as *The Fat Woman Next Door is Pregnant* (Vancouver: Talonbooks, 1981), 26.

In the five years he'd been sleeping in the same room with her, Richard had spent an incalculable number of hours watching his grandmother die. In fact, every time he examined her in her sleep, grumbling, scarcely breathing, mouth open to reveal bare white gums as sharp as knives, Richard expected to see her expire. She was an exhausted flickering candle, a dismantled gasping clock, a motor at the end of the road, a dog grown too old, a servant who had finished serving and was dying of boredom, a useless old woman, a beaten human being, his grandmother. If she wanted to do anything in the house, her daughter-in-law, the fat woman, or her daughter-in-law, Albertine, very attentively would anticipate her intentions: "You just rest...you've done enough work in your life...sit down, Momma, your leg..." The old woman would lay down the dishcloth or the wooden spoon, swallowing so she wouldn't explode. Richard had often seen his grandmother weep with rage, leaning against the window in her room that looked out on the outside staircase. He'd even heard her curse the two women, cast impotent spells on them; he'd seen her stick out her tongue and pretend to be kicking them. From morning to night, she wandered from her bedroom to the dining room, from the dining room to her bedroom, a superfluous object of attention in this house where everyone and everything had assigned tasks or at least some use—except for her.

SELECTED BIBLIOGRAPHY

Les Belles-soeurs (2nd ed., Montreal: Leméac, 1972); translated by John Van Burek and Bill Glassco (Vancouver, Talonbooks, 1974).
Bonjour, là, bonjour (Montreal: Leméac, 1974); translated by John Van Burek and Bill Glassco (Vancouver, Talonbooks, 1975).
La Grosse femme d'à côté est enceinte (Montreal: Leméac, 1978), translated by Sheila Fischman as *The Fat Woman Next Door is Pregnant*, translated by Sheila Fischman (Vancouver: Talonbooks, 1981).
Thérèse et Pierrette à l'école des Saints-Anges (Montreal: Leméac, 1978), translated by Sheila Fischman as *Thérèse et Pierrette and the Little Hanging Angel* (Toronto: McClelland & Stewart, 1984).
Douze coups de théâtre (Montreal: Leméac, 1992).

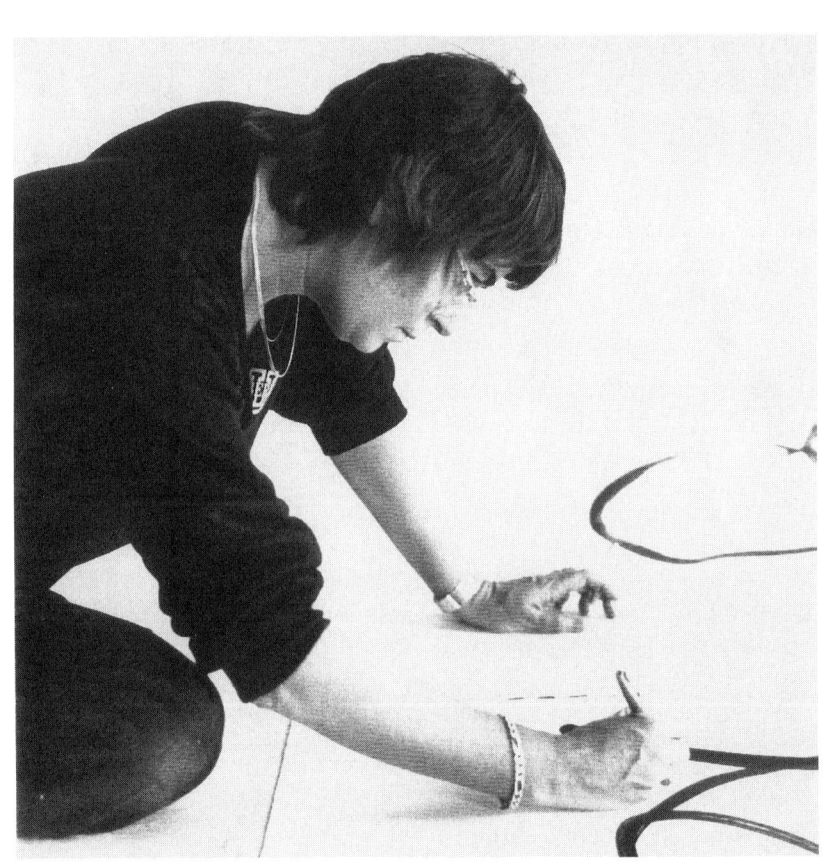

NICOLE BROSSARD

The Writer as Explorer

SHE QUESTIONS EVERYTHING. In exigent, painstaking poetry and prose, Nicole Brossard, Quebec's prize-winning postmodern feminist writer and theorist, wants to think "thoughts that have never been thought, use words in ways they have never been used." Her critically-acclaimed work defies conventional taste and throws a gauntlet at the reader in pursuit of a linear narrative thread.

Brossard was born in Montreal in 1943 ("a difficult birth where I introduced myself into this world irreverently, that is, ass first," she has written in an autobiographical essay). She grew up in the northeast section of the city on rue Grenier, moving with her family to predominantly anglophone Snowdon when she turned seven. A traditional Catholic girlhood included four years at Collège Marguerite Bourgeoys in Westmount. But an early sign of her writerly calling was the profound effect on her as a teenager of the Alain Resnais film *Nuit et brouillard* (*Night and Fog*) which depicted the mass graves found by the Allies in Auschwitz and Dachau. "I knew that never again would humanity be the same in my mind."

Attending the Université de Montréal in the mid-1960s, Brossard began publishing in the student newspaper *Le Quartier Latin* and her first poetry collection, *Aube à la saison*, appeared in 1965 when she was twenty-two. Involved in the ferment of nationalist politics, in the same year she co-founded *Barre du jour*, an avant-garde literary journal with a strong commitment to the development of Quebec literature. In 1966, she published a second book of poems and married Roger Soublières, one of the journal's other editors.

Dissociating herself from mainstream trends of 1960s Québécois poetry which focused on the land as its predominant theme, Brossard concentrated on language as a way to probe meaning and being.

After a brief stint of teaching, she decided to devote herself to full-time writing and, since the late 1960s, her output has been prolific with an oeuvre of some thirty books. Full of word play, foreign terms, and typographical devices, her work poses a formidable challenge for translators, yet, to date, seven of her novels and three poetry collections have been translated into English.

She has also co-edited an anthology of Quebec women poets, collaborated in works of theatre and documentary films, and been a prominent editor at *La Nouvelle barre du jour* and at the feminist collective *Les Têtes de pioche*.

Recognition has come in the form of two Governor General's Awards for poetry (the first in 1975 for *Mécanique jongleuse, suivi de Masculin grammaticale*; the second for *Double impression* in 1985), the Lesforges Poetry Prize, the Prix du Québec and Toronto's Harbourfront Festival Prize.

In her youth, Brossard defined herself first and foremost as a poet. (She still maintains that "a poem is a key to the interior universe.") But the experience of becoming a mother in 1974 took her by seismic force and "I understood that before anything else, I was a woman." Her subsequent work—and life—has assumed a radical feminist and lesbian orientation.

In her elegant Outremont home tucked away behind Hôpital Ste. Justine, an animated Brossard laughed with some discomfiture when I questioned her about an essay she had written about the Polytechnique Massacre of 1989. "Obviously, it has a provocative dimension," she observed, referring to a sentence in which she described walking in Paris "following my usual habit of looking only at women as if to reassure myself about humanity."

"It serves to indicate that I prefer to look on the side of women in order to have a hope in humanity, to have hope for the future." But then she added that she envisages a future in which "men will be obliged to let go a part of their aggressiveness and violence and above all of their contempt for women."

Heavily influenced by the Austrian philosopher Ludwig

Wittgenstein (who tangled with the very basic question: How is language possible, and whose "picture theory" of language is the title of a hybrid work of poetry, fiction and theory by Brossard); by the French deconstructionist philosopher Jacques Derrida; by feminist writers Gertrude Stein, Adrienne Rich and Kate Millett among others, in her later writings, Brossard has used language as a political weapon.

"You have to write two kinds of pages almost at the same time:" she told Beverley Daurio in an interview for *Books in Canada* in March 1991, "one on which you try to understand and uncover the patriarchal lies; and another on which you try to give your new values, your utopias, and everything you find positive about yourself and about women."

Brossard's novels, which deliberately subvert the familiar conventions of narrative techniques (judged to be patriarchal), are an extension of her experiments in poetry. But they also go well beyond the aims of realism that define much of traditional literature. In *The Aerial Letter*, she has written, "Reality has been for most women a fiction, and women's reality has been perceived as fiction."

In novels such as *Surfaces of Sense* and *Mauve Desert* Brossard strives, above all, to reveal the truth of women's lives. Not aspects of the truth, but the whole truth. The style of both these novels matches the audacity of the over-arching objective. *Surfaces of Sense*—reading which, for critic Beverley Daurio, "was like having my skin removed and entering another woman's body"—is replete with visual tricks that require one to read spaces on the page, ellipses and italics in order to piece together "the story" of a community of women.

Mauve Desert also explores intense relationships between a group of women in the guise of three parallel narratives (one of which is, partially, a whodunit). As cerebral as anything Brossard has written, it nevertheless transmits the passion that intersects with her theoretical systems.

"I write," she told me, "to discover, and not only to bear witness or to communicate. I write to discover new dimensions of emotions, sensations—I write to learn, to explore."

Excerpt from *Le Sens apparent*, translated by Fiona Strachan as *Sur-*

faces of Sense (Toronto: Coach House, 1989), 5.

From this moment there were double meanings and everything was in the present. A few characters, all women living in
reality, in the middle of a tender and difficult fiction which pain-
fully kept them alive.

I had also remembered several incidents which had occurred
in the course of my reflection and which, in the writing process,
could have helped me point out that the space inside mothers'
bellies has been continually expanding with the increasing number of desires. Madly, I had thought up a great love story for I
wanted to write a book, no matter what. And more. I had been
afraid of failing and that is how I had gradually turned into a sort
of narrator, always ready with appropriate examples.

Solve one problem at a time. From prose to anecdotes,
entertaining, amusing, but not, however, enough to make me
forget the fictional fire in our breasts. Several versions.

—How did Gertrude come into the world?—so real in the
ultraviolet light of appearances.

SELECTED BIBLIOGRAPHY

Mécanique jongleuse, suivi de Masculin grammaticale (Montreal: Edition
de l'Hexagone, 1974); translated by Larry Shouldice as *Daydream
Mechanics* (Toronto: Coach House Press, 1980).
L'Amèr, ou le chapitre effrité (Montreal: Quinze, 1977); translated by
Barbara Godard as *These Our Mothers, or The Disintegrating
Chapter*(Toronto: Coach House Press, 1983).
Amantes (Montreal: Quinze, 1980); translated by Barbara Godard as
Lovhers (Montreal: Guernica Press, 1986).
Le Sens apparent (Paris: Flammarion, 1980); translated by Fiona
Strachan as *Surfaces of Sense* (Toronto: Coach House Press, 1989).
Mauve Desert (Montreal: Éditions de l'Hexagone, 1987); translated
by Susanne de Lotbinière-Harwood as *Mauve Desert* (Toronto: Coach
House Press, 1990).

confidence qu'un homme était une femme
peut-être ~~l'avait-elle vraiment pensé~~ *le pense-t-elle vraiment*

*pour concevoir dans sa langue le
mobile ~~plus~~ qu'il expose l'entre le mental et
~~les phrases~~ sonores complètes ~~le~~
~~grand tout se joue dans l'ombre~~
~~prépare seule que pousse de lumière~~
cohérente s'apparente au projet
de (Michèle Vaillancourt) et*

*si l'on songe qu'une source de lumière
cohérente s'apparente au projet
de la voir venir version lisse
Oriana Longari ~~dans (~~~~)~~ contemporaines, son souffle un tourment
tout le corps y passe pour un son
songe la légende dérive en un
texte la musique ~~une~~ image qui
l'accompagne la cascade de l'histoire
dans l'histoire éclatée les phrases
~~cette s'explient à~~ s'ouvriraient*

phrase
*j'énonce
d'une idée*

l'idée

*peau la
image*

*legenda : ce qui
doit être lu*

*amplifié par
l'imagination .*

*tout texte qui accompagne
une image et lui donne
un sens .*

. liste explicative

Manuscript page, Nicole Brossard

189

Credits

Page 20, National Archives of Canada C-47354; 26, Bibaud: Bibliothèque nationale du Québec; 30, Viger: Bibliothèque nationale du Québec; 34, Leprohon: cover, Department of Rare Books and Special Collections, McGill University Libraries; photo, courtesy of Antoinette Leprohon Fitzsimons; 38, McGee: Concordia University Archives; 42, Fréchette: Bibliothèque nationale du Québec; 46, Nelligan: (about 40 years old) Bibliothèque nationale du Québec; 50, Leacock: photo, McGill University Archives; 55, manuscript, Department of Rare Books and Special Collections, McGill University Libraries; 56, Ringuet: Department of Rare Books and Special Collections, McGill University Libraries; 60, Graham: Department of Rare Books and Special Collections, McGill University Libraries; 64, Klein: photo by Federal Photos (1951) Canadian Jewish Congress Archives; 70, Scott: courtesy of Aileen Collins and Louis Dudek; 75, photo by Tim Clark (Irving Layton, F. R. Scott & Louis Dudek, 5 March 1983), courtesy of Nancy Marrelli and Simon Dardick; 76, Thériault: Bibliothèque nationale du Québec with the permission of Michel Thériault; 82, Aquin: Bibliothèque nationale du Québec; 88, Roy: *Montreal Gazette*; 94 MacLennan: McGill University Archives; 100, Gélinas: photo of Gélinas as Tit-Coq; 105, program for *Tit-Coq*, Concordia University Archives with permission of Gratien Gélinas; 106, Layton: courtesy of Sam Tata; 112, Dudek: (photo circa 1952) courtesy of Louis Dudek; 117, manuscript courtesy of Louis Dudek; 118, Gallant: photo by Geoff Isherwood, 123, cover, Random House, 1986; 124, Kattani photo (Baghdad, 1946); 129, manuscript, courtesy of Naïm Kattan; 130, Hood: photo by Lois Seigal (1988 QSPELL Awards); 136, Richler: photo by Lois Seigal; 142, Cohen: sheet music courtesy Concordia University Archives; 148, 153, Carrier: Bibliothèque nationale du Québec; 154, Blais: photo by Claire Ramat; 160, Marchessault: photo by Algis Kemezys, courtesy of Leméac; 166, Ducharme: Éditions du Belier; 172, 177, Beauchemin: photo by Kèro, courtesy of Yves Beauchemin; 178, Tremblay: photo by Les Papparazzi, courtesy of Agence Goodwin; 184, Brossard: (working in studio of artist Françine Simonin, 1982) photo by Monique Crouillère, courtesy Nicole Brossard; 192, manuscript courtesy of Nicole Brossard.

Celebrating Twenty Years
1973-1993